THE FLAVOURS OF

FRANCE

FABULOUS VEGETARIAN CUISINE
FOR EVERY OCCASION

Master Chef Jean Conil and Fay Franklin

Angus&Robertson
An imprint of HarperCollinsPublishers

Angus&Robertson
An imprint of HarperCollins*Publishers*

First published in Australia in 1995

Copyright © HarperCollins*Publishers* Pty Limited, Australia, 1995

HarperCollins*Publishers*
25 Ryde Road, Pymble, Sydney, NSW 2073, Australia
31 View Road, Glenfield, Auckland 10, New Zealand
77–85 Fulham Palace Road, London W6 8JB, United Kingdom
Hazelton Lanes, 55 Avenue Road, Suite 2900, Toronto, Ontario M5R 3L2
and 1995 Markham Road, Scarborough, Ontario M1B 5M8, Canada
10 East 53rd Street, New York NY 10032, USA

National Library of Australia Cataloguing-in-Publication data:

Conil, Jean.
    The Flavours of France
    Includes index.

    ISBN 0 207 18846 7.1.
    Vegetarian cookery. 2. Cookery, French. I. Franklin, Fay. I
    I Title.

641.5636

Photography by Andrew Elton
Food prepared and styled for photography by Lynne Mullins, assisted by Emma Thomas
Design by Kerry Klinner

Printed in Hong Kong

9 8 7 6 5 4 3 2 1
95 96 97 98 99
Cover photograph: *Onion Tart (p. 63)*
Page 1 photograph: *Tomatoes Stuffed with Goat's Cheese, Nuts, and Garlic (p. 24)*
Page 3 photograph: *Parisian Cigarettes (p. 154)*
Page 4 and 5 photograph: *Lemony Vegetable Soup with Cream (left) (p. 47),*
Gratin of Broccoli and Potatoes (below left)(p. 85),
and Apple Flan, Normandy Style (right)(p. 128)
Page 6 and 7 photograph: *Pumpkin Soup (p. 40)*
Lynne Mullins and the Publishers would like to thank the following contributors
for generously supplying props for photography:
Accoutrement, Mosman and Gordon, NSW
Country Road, Australia
Wendy Schmidt, Greenwich, NSW
Kitchen Kapers, Crows Nest, NSW
Your Display Gallery, Greenwich, NSW

Acknowledgments

I am much indebted to the women who influenced me to become a chef, and the women who encouraged me to adopt the principle of pleasing, as a matter of policy, by cooking their favorite dishes.

My gratitude goes to my maternal grandmother, Mathilde, who was a keen gardener and who taught me how to grow vegetables and cook them to perfection; to my mother, Marie-José, who demanded a hot or cold vegetable starter for every meal; to my late wife, Mary, who was Irish and whose potato dishes were a meal in themselves; to my daughter, Patricia, who was one of my many pupils and whose repertoire of fruit mousse recipes reads like poetry; to my Irish sister-in-law, Kitty, who helped me entertain our international culinary colleagues regularly; and not least to my collaborator, Fay Franklin, who has interpreted the spirit of French gastronomy with talent and taste.

Indeed, I thank all my many female fans around the world who have been my faithful customers in the top restaurants where I have been employed. It is because of them I have enjoyed creating new vegetarian dishes good enough to become classics in a world of novelty and universal diets.

Master Chef Jean Conil, 1995

CONTENTS

DES MATIÈRES

INTRODUCTION

It is now over a decade since we first introduced the concept of Cuisine Végétarienne Française. At that time, many people chuckled and said that the very idea of French and vegetarian cuisines coming together was ridiculous. How wrong they were. Perhaps they did not realise how times were changing – that there were growing numbers of vegetarians around who really loved good food; that there were many more people who were seeking to cut down on their consumption of meat, but did not want to relinquish taste for the sake of, say, health; that good caterers and restaurateurs were looking for ways to respond to their customers' wishes for meat-free meals without resorting to the old stand-bys of omelet and salad.

True, you will still find few exclusively vegetarian restaurants in France; true, there are still those establishments that, amazingly, think we will accept as vegetables a side order of watery, processed peas and anemic, tasteless, steamed potatoes. But we chose to draw the majority of the recipes in this book not from catering manuals, but from the traditional recipes of the French people themselves, and from the farmhouse kitchens, market gardens, and homely *auberges* (inns) of the French countryside. Good chefs all over the world are doing likewise – the *cuisine du terroir*, cooking of the land, is as influential today as *nouvelle cuisine* was when we first began to write about French vegetarian food.

France is still an agricultural country, and many of its people have lived off the land for generations. When meat was scarce, they turned to the produce of their fields and forests for sustenance. They never compromised on flavor or freshness (and neither should you). Because of this history, many traditional 'peasant' dishes are fundamentally vegetarian – there is even a fish-free bouillabaisse! At the other end of the scale, think of the classic dishes like cheese soufflé or Dauphinoise potatoes, which are far removed from the late and unlamented nut cutlet, and yet they are just as uncompromisingly vegetarian.

Typically, the towns in France where vegetarian restaurants can be found are those with a large student population. In that respect, France is like the rest of the world. It has been the young people who have most enthusiastically embraced the idea of meat-free eating over the last decade. And, since they carry with them no outdated images of what vegetarian food 'ought' to be like, they have shaped and influenced what it is now becoming – adventurous, imaginative and positively chic! One could compare the phenomenon to that of New World wines, for so long scorned in comparison to the great Bordeaux and Burgundies of France, it just needed some enthusiastic individuals, with no preconceptions but plenty of new ideas, to produce wines which now rank as classics in their own right, not pale imitations of old styles.

Young diners and cooks no longer see the aforementioned nut cutlet as their only option. They know there is better to be had, and they are confident enough to demand it. So, it is for them, above all, that we have created this book, because they are the future of good vegetarian food.

Compiling this book from a decade's worth of research and recipes was easy – if anything, we were spoilt for choice in selecting from such a wealth of dishes. We have tried to balance new with old, family cooking with fare for special occasions. We have attempted to match the best of what emerged from *nouvelle cuisine* with dishes that have evolved over centuries. We hope that what you read will inspire you, and give you many delicious meals and happy memories.

Jean Conil and Fay Franklin

Cold Appetizers

Les Hors d'Oeuvres Froids

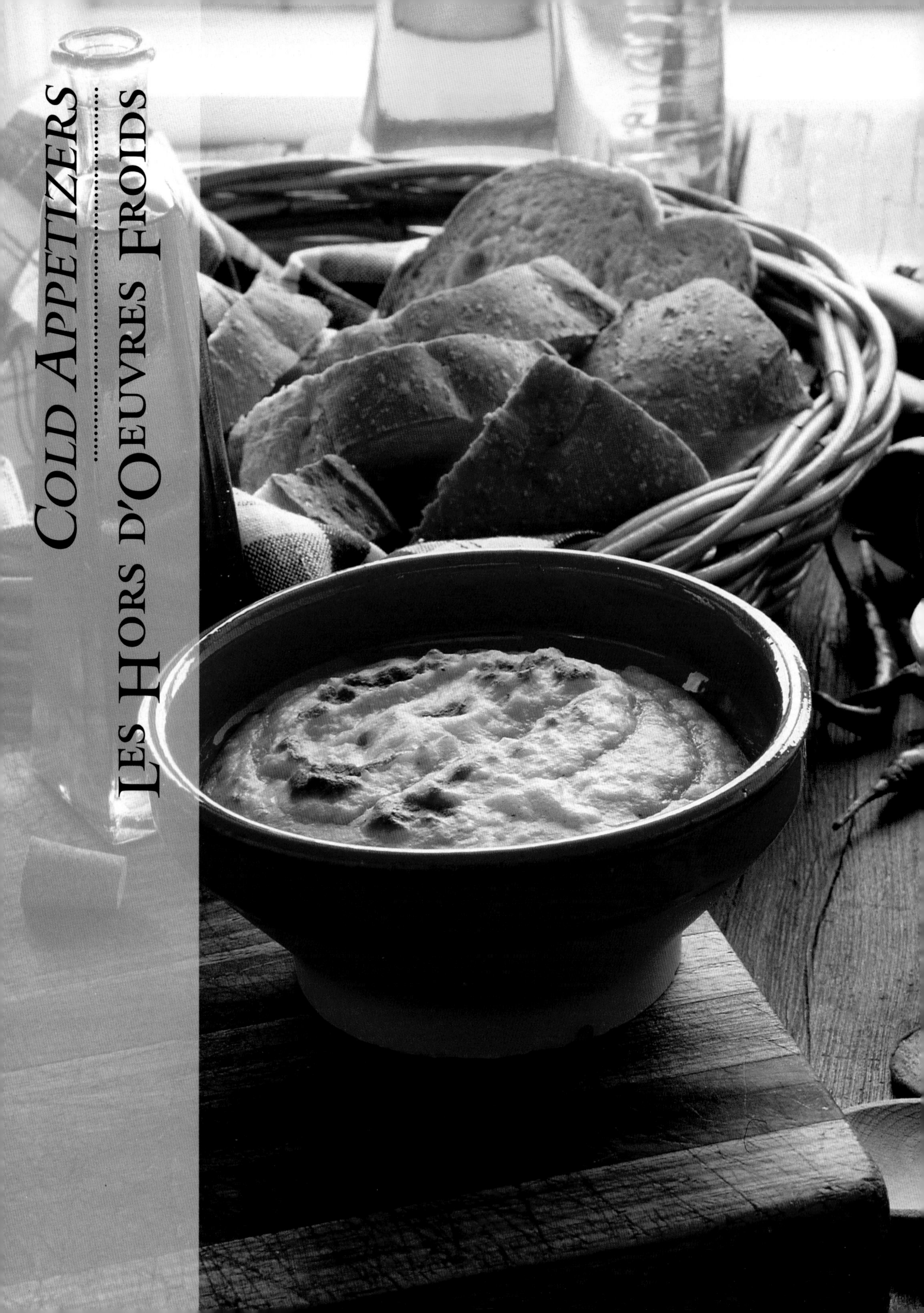

Black Olive Tapénade

La Tapéna aux Olives Noires

In Greece the olive tree is a symbol of wisdom, abundance and, as everyone knows, peace. In cooking the olive is a fruit that lends itself to many inventive uses. By far the best, to my mind, is that delicious Mediterranean pâté known as tapénade. It is usually made with anchovies, but my version, with walnuts, is more delicate in flavor.

2 cups (8 oz., 250 g) large black olives, pitted*
1¾ cups (8 oz., 250 g) shelled walnuts
¼ cup (2 oz., 60 g) large pickled capers
4 hard-boiled egg yolks (and whites, if desired)
4 raw egg yolks
1 small green chili pepper
2 garlic cloves
pinch of grated nutmeg *or* mace
2 tablespoons soy sauce
2 tablespoons wine vinegar
1 tablespoon yeast extract
¼ cup (2 fl. oz., 60 ml) olive oil
pinch of dried tarragon
1 teaspoon Demerara (raw) sugar *or* molasses
(dark treacle)
freshly ground black pepper

Put all the ingredients in a food processor or blender and blend to a paste. Alternatively, mince the ingredients to a coarse paste, then beat until thoroughly combined.

This pâté will keep well in the refrigerator. Serve on whole-wheat (wholemeal) toast or as a filling for tomatoes or cucumbers. For a lighter batter, add ½ cup (4 fl. oz., 125 ml) whipped light cream. The dish can then be served as a dip.

* Most good kitchen supplies shops sell a device for removing the stones from small fruits such as olives or cherries.

SERVES 4

Pictured on previous pages: Black Olive Tapénade, Eggplant Dip, and Lentil Pâté

Eggplant Dip

Caviar d'Aubergines

The eggplant (aubergine) is a member of the nightshade family and, naturally, has an affinity with other members of the same family, in particular tomatoes, peppers, and potatoes. Although the eggplant has always been popular in France, it has only become widely available in some countries comparatively recently, initially through specialist ethnic shops.
Eggplant contains bitter juices which, in most cases, should be drawn out. To do this, sprinkle slices of the vegetable with salt, leave for 30 minutes, then rinse in cold water. The technique I use in this recipe makes this rather laborious first step unnecessary.
A leading Lebanese restaurateur and chef told me that he likes to serve his version of this pâté with a garnish of eggplant fritters. To prepare these, the slices must be salted as described above, dried, dipped in egg and either flour, breadcrumbs, or nuts, and deep-fried. The fritters can then be dipped in the pâté and eaten.

3 eggplants (aubergines) (about 1½ lbs., 750 g),
pricked all over with a fork
4 medium eggs, hard-boiled and chopped
8 oz. (250 g) tomatoes, peeled, deseeded,
and quartered
1 large onion, chopped
1 cup (8 fl. oz., 250 ml) olive oil *or* a mixture of
melted butter and olive oil
2 garlic cloves, finely chopped
1 teaspoon sea salt
freshly ground black pepper
juice of ½ lemon
¼ cup (2 fl. oz., 60 ml) tahini

Put the eggplants in an oven preheated at 400°F (200°C). Bake until soft — about 20 to 25 minutes. Set aside.

When the eggplants are cool enough to handle, peel and reserve the pulp.

Combine the pulp, eggs, tomatoes, onion, oil, and garlic in a food processor or blender until it forms a purée. Season with salt and pepper, add the lemon juice and tahini, and chill for 1 hour before serving.

Variation

For a thicker paste, to serve as a pâté rather than a dip, add 1 level tablespoon arrowroot mixed in ⅔ cup (5 fl. oz., 155 ml) cold water. Stir this into the eggplant purée. Heat the mixture to boiling point and boil for 4 minutes to cook the starch and thicken the batter to the right consistency.

SERVES 4

LENTIL PÂTÉ

PÂTÉ DE LENTILLES D'ÉSAÜ

The red pottage for which Esau sold his birthright is said to have been made from split red lentils. Whether whole or split, or reduced to a flour, lentils are exceedingly nutritious. In the past, they always needed a thorough inspection before cooking — nevertheless, it was common to break a tooth on a small stone lurking in the dish. Modern methods remove most of the impurities before packaging, but you should still check for grit if at all doubtful.

1 cup (8 oz., 250 g) red lentils, picked over

6 oz. (185 g) potatoes, peeled and sliced

6 oz. (185 g) onions, chopped

6 oz. (185 g) carrots, peeled and sliced

good pinch of dried thyme

3 eggs

good pinch of ground cumin

2 teaspoons sea salt

1 teaspoon Demerara (raw) sugar

freshly ground black pepper

2 garlic cloves, peeled

2 oz. (60 g) butter *or* oil

Wash the lentils, then soak for a minimum of 6 hours or overnight.

Drain the lentils and place in a saucepan. Just cover with cold water and add the potatoes, onions, carrots, and thyme. Boil for 25 minutes. Drain, then dry off the vegetables and lentils by cooking over a very low heat for about 4 minutes.

Mash with a Mouli grater or potato masher until the mixture forms a coarse purée.

Beat the eggs with the cumin, salt, sugar, and pepper in a large bowl, then add the purée.

Blend the garlic and butter or oil in a food processor or blender. Stir into the mixture.

Place the mixture in an earthenware baking dish and bake for 20 minutes at 400°F (200°C) until golden brown on top. Chill and serve with whole-wheat (wholemeal) bread.

SERVES 4

WALNUT PÂTÉ

LA PÂTÉ AUX NOIX DE PUISLAURENT

Shelled walnuts go rancid very quickly, so they are best bought whole to guarantee freshness. To develop good flavor from shelled kernels, sauté for a minute in walnut or olive oil, then drain on kitchen paper.

2/3 cup (5 fl. oz., 155 ml) vegetable oil, preferably walnut

1/2 cup (4 oz., 125 g) chopped celery

4 oz. (125 g) onions, finely chopped

4 oz. (125 g) carrots, finely chopped

2 oz. (60 g) mushrooms, chopped

2 cups (8 oz., 250 g) walnut kernels

1 cup (8 oz., 250 g) brown rice

2½ cups (1 imp. pint, 625 ml) water

juice and grated rind of 1 lemon

2 garlic cloves

1 tablespoon active dry yeast

2 eggs, beaten

1/2 cup (2 oz., 60 g) pickled walnuts and 1 tablespoon pickling juice

2 oz. (60 g) curd cheese

1 teaspoon clear honey

1/4 cup (2 fl. oz., 60 ml) Marsala

sea salt and freshly ground black pepper

good pinch each of ground mace and ginger

Heat the oil in a saucepan and stir-fry the vegetables and walnut kernels for 5 minutes. Add the rice and sauté for a further 4 minutes. Stir in the water and boil gently for 45 minutes, with the lid on, until the rice is soft. Drain any liquid and reserve. Mince or blend this mixture to a purée. Set aside.

If there is any liquid left from the rice (there should be no more than ⅔ cup (5 fl. oz., 155 ml)), place it in a food processor or blender, along with the lemon juice and rind, garlic, yeast, eggs, pickled walnuts and juice, curd cheese, honey, and Marsala. Blend thoroughly.

Combine the rice and vegetable purée with this mixture and stir together well. Season with salt, pepper, mace, and ginger. Pour the mixture into an oiled 8-in. (20-cm) loaf pan and bake at 400°F (200°C) for 45 minutes. Chill.

To serve, cut the pâté into thick slices and garnish with celery and scallions (spring onions). Serve with crackers or toasted whole-wheat (wholemeal) French bread.

SERVES 4

FIELD MUSHROOM 'CAVIAR'

LE CAVIAR DES CHAMPIGNONS DE PRAIRIE

The field mushroom is the best variety to use for this dish. It has a better flavor for grilling or cooked dishes than the white cultivated variety.

4 oz. (125 g) butter
1 cup (6 oz., 185 g) chopped onion
1 lb. (500 g) field mushrooms with stalks, trimmed and finely chopped
1 cup (2 oz., 60 g) soft whole-wheat (wholemeal) breadcrumbs
1 garlic clove, peeled
juice of ½ lemon
⅓ cup (3 fl. oz., 90 ml) Marsala, sherry, *or* dry vermouth
2 tablespoons chopped fresh parsley
1 tablespoon cornstarch (cornflour)
½ cup (4 fl. oz., 125 ml) heavy *or* sour cream
1 teaspoon sea salt
large pinch of freshly ground black pepper
4 oz. (125 g) curd cheese
large pinch of ground mace
pinch of ground thyme

Heat the butter in a saucepan and gently sauté the onion until light brown, then add the chopped mushrooms. Literally boil them down until almost all their moisture has evaporated, then add the breadcrumbs.

Blend the garlic with the lemon juice, Marsala, and parsley in a food processor or blender and stir into the mushrooms. Boil for 5 minutes.

Combine the cornstarch and cream together in a bowl. Stir this into the mushroom purée to thicken. Simmer for 5 minutes, season with salt and pepper, then cool.

In a bowl, beat the mushroom purée well with the curd cheese. Add the mace and thyme, and stir thoroughly.

Arrange the pâté on individual serving plates. Chill, then serve with hot, fried bread cut into triangles or fingers.

VARIATIONS

For a white pâté, use cultivated white mushrooms, but wash them well and blanch in water and lemon juice beforehand. This pâté is an ideal filling for tomatoes, zucchini (courgettes), or little pie shells.

For a Mediterranean flavor, decorate your pâté with black olives, walnut halves, and marinated button mushrooms.

SERVES 4

AVOCADO AND TOMATO DIP

LE PÂTÉ D'AVOCAT AUX TOMATES

The avocado is a fruit. It was once served only as an exotic starter with half a lemon or lime, or a vinaigrette sauce, or with cooked, chilled shrimp, lobster, or crab meat. Nowadays, chefs are inventing new uses for this versatile ingredient: it can be made into a dip or a soup; diluted as a sauce; or peeled and sliced with tomatoes and peppers as a salad. The avocado is rich in fat, which is polyunsaturated for the most part and so less harmful. It is high in protein compared with other fruits, and has small amounts of vitamin A and vitamin C.
Some chefs add whipped light whipping cream to the pulp to create a mousse. Others simply flavor the strained pulp with a little lemon juice, chopped onion, sea salt, and black pepper. I have found that a little cooked spinach improves both the color and the vitamin content of the pulp.
This pâté includes low-fat cream cheese, a bland flavor that marries well with that of the avocado. It is given its piquancy by the addition of tomato paste (purée) and lemon juice. Because avocado tends to discolor quite quickly, it is advisable to prepare it at the last minute.

2 ripe avocados (1 lb., 500 g approximately)
2 tomatoes, peeled, seeded, and chopped
1 tablespoon tomato paste (purée)
juice and grated rind of 1 lemon
1 garlic clove
1 small onion, chopped
¼ cup (2 oz., 60 g) chopped, cooked spinach
8 oz. (250 g) curd cheese
1 teaspoon sea salt
good pinch of paprika
freshly ground black pepper

Peel the avocados and push through a strainer to make a smooth paste.

Blend the tomatoes, tomato paste, lemon juice and rind, garlic, onion, and spinach in a blender or food processor.

In a large bowl, combine all ingredients and season to taste. Transfer to four individual bowls and chill for 1 hour, covered with waxed paper.

Serve with crudités (sticks of carrot, celery, pepper, etc.) or crackers. It can also be used as a stuffing for small tomatoes.

SERVES 4

Pictured opposite: Field Mushroom 'Caviar', and Avocado and Tomato Dip

ROQUEFORT CHEESE PÂTÉ WITH CELERIAC

LE PÂTÉ DE ROQUEFORT AU CELERI-RAVE

Roquefort cheese has been made in the little village of Roquefort for over 2000 years. It is one of the finest cheeses in the world and is copied by many Western countries, with varying degrees of success. The best is England's kingly Stilton, followed by the blue cheeses of Denmark, and Italy's pungent Gorgonzola. Any of these cheeses can be used in this recipe. The blue streaks are due to Penicillium roqueforti or P. glaucum, molds obtained from wheat and barley.
The recipe for this pâté is an ideal way of using up odds and ends of cheese left over from a dinner party.

8 oz. (250 g) celeriac, peeled and sliced
4 oz. (125 g) cream cheese
8 oz. (250 g) Roquefort cheese
good pinch each of grated nutmeg and celery seeds
freshly ground black pepper
1 teaspoon sea salt
1 tablespoon chopped fresh parsley *or* coriander
1/3 cup (3 fl. oz., 90 ml) ruby port

Put the celeriac in a saucepan and just cover with water. Boil for 10 minutes or until soft. Drain, then push through a strainer to form a purée.

Mix the purée with the cream cheese and Roquefort. Reheat to bubbling point, then either blend or pass through the strainer again. Allow to cool.

When cold, season with nutmeg, celery seeds, salt, and pepper. Add the parsley and port and stir well.

Serve in individual bowls. Garnish with celery and serve with whole-wheat (wholemeal) toast.

Note: Celeriac is the name given to the root of a celery-flavored umbelliferous plant. Its flavor is well complemented by other strong flavors, such as blue cheese.

The French are very fond of celeriac in salads. The root is peeled and washed, then sliced and immersed in cold water with lemon juice to keep it white. The slices are cut into thin strips or grated, then blended with a mustardy mayonnaise. This makes a delicious salad on its own or as part of an *hors d'oeuvre*. The seeds and leaves of the plant are used as a flavoring in soups and stews.

SERVES 4

BROCCOLI AND CAULIFLOWER PÂTÉ

LE PÂTÉ AUX DEUX CHOU-FLEURS

Many people need to be reintroduced to cauliflower in its 'gourmet' forms — raw with dips, marinated in a vinaigrette, or lightly steamed until just tender. Eating it this way is a delightful experience.
Broccoli is much the same. Its delicate flavor should be treated with care and is enhanced when served like asparagus, with a vinaigrette or a hollandaise sauce. Cauliflower and broccoli complement each other well, particularly in this subtly flavored pâté.

1/2 cup (4 fl. oz., 125 ml) peanut oil
8 oz. (250 g) cauliflower, divided into florets
4 oz. (125 g) onions, chopped
1 green and 1 red sweet pepper (capsicum), deseeded and chopped
8 oz. (250 g) potatoes, peeled and cut into small cubes
good pinch each of ginger, mace, turmeric, black pepper, and paprika
1/4 cup (2 oz., 60 g) tomato paste (purée)
8 oz. (250 g) broccoli
juice and grated rind of 1 lemon
2 garlic cloves, peeled
5 oz. (155 g) curd cheese
4 eggs, beaten
sea salt to taste
1/2 cup (2 oz., 60 g) grated cheese

Heat the oil and stir-fry the cauliflower with the onion, peppers, and potato cubes for 5 minutes. Sprinkle on the spices, add the tomato paste, and mix well. Add about 2½ cups (1 imp. pint, 625 ml) water and boil for 15 to 20 minutes until the vegetables are cooked.

Drain the vegetables, reserving the cooking liquid in a saucepan.

Add the broccoli to this reserved liquid and boil for 12 minutes.

Drain the cooking liquid into a food processor or blender. Add the lemon juice and rind, garlic, and curd cheese. Blend to a thin purée. Stir into the cauliflower and potato mixture.

Stir the eggs into the mixture. Add salt to taste.

Dice or roughly chop the broccoli and add to the mixture. Place in an earthenware baking dish and sprinkle the grated cheese over the top.

Bake at 400°F (200°C) for 45 minutes. Chill. Serve with fresh whole-wheat (wholemeal) bread or warm toast.

Pictured right: Crêpe-lined Vegetable and Sour Cream Loaf

SERVES 4

CRÊPE-LINED VEGETABLE AND SOUR CREAM LOAF

TERRINE DE LÉGUMES PICARDIE

This dish will appeal to the adventurous cook. The result is visually attractive, and the combination of flavors and textures will delight guests at a special dinner party.

4 leeks (white part only), trimmed
4 turnips, cut in 2-in. (5-cm) matchsticks
4 carrots, cut in 2-in. (5-cm) matchsticks

1 quantity crêpe batter (see p. 152)

LOAF FILLING
3 oz. (90 g) margarine *or* butter
1/2 cup (2 oz., 60 g) grated cheese
1/2 cup (4 fl. oz., 125 ml) sour cream
2 eggs, beaten
sea salt and freshly ground black pepper
2 garlic cloves, chopped
1 small onion, chopped
4 oz. (125 g) new potatoes, boiled and diced

Boil the leeks until just cooked. Boil the turnips for 4 minutes and the carrots for 5 minutes. Set all vegetables aside to cool.

Make 4 even-sized crêpes.

Grease a loaf pan with the margarine or butter, then line it with three of the crêpes. Trim the fourth so that it will neatly cover the top of the pan, but set it aside for the moment.

To make the filling, mix the cheese, sour cream, eggs, salt, pepper, garlic, and onions together in a bowl. Stir in the potatoes.

In the bottom of the lined pan, place one of the leeks. Flank with a row of turnip sticks on one side and carrot sticks on the other. Cover with a layer of sour cream and potato filling. Repeat this procedure until all the ingredients are used. Top with the reserved crêpe, as a lid, and brush this with a little melted butter.

Bake the loaf at 400°F (200°C) for 45 minutes. Cool and turn out onto a serving dish. Serve accompanied by a raw tomato salad with a French dressing, which could be arranged attractively around the loaf. When the loaf is sliced, the rows of colored vegetables in the pale creamy potato filling will form a decorative pattern.

SERVES 4

GREEN PEA, LETTUCE, AND ONION PÂTÉ

Le Pâté Clamart

In England, pease pudding and mushy peas are traditional favorites, yet for some reason, 'fresh' peas are expected to be vivid green and tasting of nothing but mint. In France flavor comes before color and, hence, Petits Pois à la Française (see p. 83), gently cooked with tiny onions, lettuce, and butter, is a classic vegetable dish. I have combined the traditional pea purée of England with this famous French recipe to create a dish to delight all nations!

1¹/₃ cups (8 oz., 250 g) shelled peas

¹/₂ lettuce, grated

4 oz. (125 g) button onions, peeled and blanched

2 oz. (60 g) butter

¹/₂ cup (2 oz., 60 g) whole-wheat (wholemeal) flour

2 eggs, beaten

4 oz. (125 g) curd cheese

sea salt and freshly ground black pepper

1 teaspoon Demerara (raw) sugar *or* honey

Put the peas, lettuce, and onions in a saucepan and just cover with water. Boil until the peas are tender — about 20 minutes. Drain, reserving the liquid.

Make a butter paste by creaming the softened butter and the flour.

Reheat the cooking liquid to boiling point and thicken it by adding the paste bit by bit until a sauce forms. Whisk the sauce so that it is perfectly smooth. Allow to cool for 5 minutes.

Combine the eggs and curd cheese together.

Mince or mash the pea mixture and the sauce to a purée. Stir this into the egg and cheese mixture. Add seasoning and sugar.

Reheat the batter until it begins to bubble, stirring constantly. The heat will cook the eggs, binding the pâté. Chill and serve with whole-wheat (wholemeal) bread, or serve hot on sippets of fried whole-wheat (wholemeal) bread.

VARIATION
Fresh spinach leaves can be used as a substitute for the lettuce.

SERVES 4

Pictured opposite: Marinade of Mixed Vegetables in a Lemon-Wine Dressing

MARINADE OF MIXED VEGETABLES IN A LEMON–WINE DRESSING

Marinade de Légumes au Vin Blanc

This dish is not quite a pickle but will keep for a week if refrigerated. It is delicious with hard-boiled eggs or hard cheeses, or good on its own, with just a hunk of bread. Fennel, leeks, white radishes, and artichoke bases can also be prepared this way.

MARINADE
2¹/₂ cups (1 imp. pint, 625 ml) half water, half dry white wine

1 bay leaf

1 sprig thyme

²/₃ cup (5 fl. oz., 155 ml) olive oil

juice and grated rind of 2 lemons

3 tablespoons white wine vinegar

6 coriander seeds

2 chili peppers

4 black peppercorns, lightly crushed

2 tablespoons chopped fresh ginger

1 tablespoon sea salt

2 teaspoons turmeric

2 garlic cloves, chopped

1 tablespoon Demerara (raw) sugar

VEGETABLES
12 button mushrooms, whole or halved

3 carrots, peeled and cut into sticks 2 in. x ¹/₄ in. (5 cm x 6 mm) or thin slices

4 celery sticks

3 small turnips, peeled and cut into sticks 2 in. x ¹/₄ in. (5 cm x 6 mm) or thin slices

12 button onions, peeled

1 small cauliflower, divided into florets

In a large saucepan, boil together all the marinade ingredients for 5 minutes.

Wipe clean the mushrooms, stalks trimmed if needed, and put in cold water with lemon juice.

Boil the carrots and celery for 5 minutes. Add the turnips, onions, and cauliflower and cook for a further 4 minutes. Add the mushrooms and cook for 1 minute more.

Drain the cooked vegetables and place in the marinade. Allow to cool, then refrigerate for 24 hours. The vegetables will retain their crispness when removed from the marinade and served.

SERVES 4

FLAGEOLET BEAN DIP FROM BRITTANY

PÂTÉ DE FLAGEOLET BRETONNE

Flageolets are the youngest seeds from the finest variety of haricot beans, gathered and shelled while they are still a pale, delicate shade of green. Dried flageolet beans are sold in most health food shops. They must be soaked overnight. Some tap water contains minerals, which can make beans tough. Adding a little baking soda (bicarbonate of soda) to the water will help, but distilled water will give the best results. Wash the soaked beans in fresh water before cooking.

The traditional method of baking beans in a casserole takes from 1½ to 2 hours — chickpeas (garbanzos) can take as long as 3½ hours. If you are in a hurry, most beans take only 20 minutes to cook in a pressure cooker. Or take the short cut of using canned beans, which are available in convenient 'catering' sizes as well as standard sizes. Even the finest chefs rarely bake their own beans these days.

2 garlic cloves, peeled
juice of ½ lemon
1 cup (8 oz., 250 g) tinned flageolet beans, drained
½ cup (4 fl. oz., 125 ml) olive oil *or* melted good-quality butter
pinch each of cayenne pepper and ground coriander
1 small onion, finely chopped
1 tablespoon tomato paste (purée)
1 teaspoon sea salt
freshly ground black pepper
½ teaspoon Demerara (raw) sugar

In a blender or food processor, blend the garlic with the lemon juice. Add all the remaining ingredients and blend to a smooth purée.

Chill the pâté for an hour and serve with matzo or water biscuits, and a platter of strips of root vegetables, cucumber, whole radishes, cauliflower florets, mushrooms, celery, and curly endive.

Note: If the batter is too stiff, add a little whipped light whipping cream. If it is too soft, add a little cream cheese.

Red or black kidney beans, cannellini beans, lima (butter) beans, and chickpeas can be prepared in the same way.

The pâté will keep well in the refrigerator, and can be frozen. It can be spread on bread or toast, or used in sandwiches.

SERVES 4

Pictured above right: Asparagus Mousse 'Mimosa'

ARTICHOKES IN A FRENCH DRESSING ENRICHED WITH EGGS

ARTICHAUT, SAUCE GRIBICHE

The artichoke is one of the oldest cultivated vegetables. The base is the most solid edible part, but the leaves also have a small portion of edible flesh where they attach to the body of the plant. Once boiled in acidulated water to prevent discoloration, this part of the leaf is tender and quite delicious when dipped in dressings.

Mature artichokes have an inedible, thistly part above the heart called the 'choke', which must be carefully removed. In Italy, where young artichokes are eaten, the whole plant can be used, as the choke has not yet formed.

4 artichokes
4 slices lemon
2 tablespoons olive oil
1 tablespoon whole-wheat (wholemeal) flour
juice of 1 lemon
good pinch of sea salt
1 quantity Herb Sauce with Egg (see p. 172)

Hold the artichoke firmly with one hand and snap the stem sharply downwards with the other. Using a very sharp stainless steel knife, in a curving motion, cut off all the bottom leaves to trim the base of the artichoke neatly without exposing the white flesh. Tie a slice of lemon to the base with string. Repeat for the remaining three artichokes.

Neatly trim 1 in. (2 cm) off the top of the upper leaves with a pair of scissors. This helps when removing the choke later.

To prevent the artichokes discoloring, prepare a blanching liquid. Cream together the oil and flour with the lemon juice. Add this and the salt to 7 cups (3 imp. pints, 1.75 litres) water. Bring to the boil and drop in the artichokes. Cook for 35 minutes.

Drain the cooked artichokes and refresh under running water until cold. Carefully remove the choke so the heart is exposed. Place each artichoke in an individual serving dish.

Serve the individual artichokes with a bowl of Herb Sauce with Egg on the side.

Note: Artichokes have a better flavor when cold, but if you wish to try them hot for a change, serve with a sharper sauce, such as Shallot Cream Sauce (see p. 172).

SERVES 4

ASPARAGUS MOUSSE 'MIMOSA'

....

MOUSSE D'ASPERGES MIMOSA

*'Mimosa' is the term used when a dish is garnished with
chopped egg yolk. The very pale green of this mousse is
complemented by the egg's yellow, and the colors seem to
suit that wonderful time in spring when asparagus
becomes plentiful — and affordable!*

8 oz. (250 g) thin asparagus spears, trimmed

²/₃ cup (5 fl. oz., 155 ml) milk

2 small shallots, finely chopped

5 teaspoons agar-agar

sea salt and freshly ground black pepper

pinch of grated nutmeg

2 eggs, hard-boiled and chopped

²/₃ cup (5 fl. oz., 155 ml) heavy cream

¹/₃ cup (3 fl. oz., 90 ml) Vinaigrette (see p. 168)

Bring a large saucepan of salted water to the
boil. Drop in the asparagus spears and cook
for about 5 minutes or until they are bright green
and tender. Refresh under cold running water,
then drain well.

In another saucepan, heat the milk and the
shallots. Dissolve the agar-agar in the milk and
bring to the boil. Simmer for 8 minutes. Remove
from the heat and allow to cool slightly.

Roughly chop the asparagus, reserving 4 good
tips for a garnish. Add the rest to the milk and
season to taste with salt, pepper, and nutmeg.
Purée until smooth and creamy. Allow to cool.

Peel and finely chop the eggs. Add to the
mixture, reserving a little for a garnish. Whip the
cream lightly and stir into the mixture.

Line four medium-sized ramekins with oiled
plastic wrap and divide the mixture evenly
between them. Cover and refrigerate for at least
2 hours or until set.

To serve, unmold the mousses onto individual
serving plates (the plastic wrap will make this
easy). Drizzle each one with a little vinaigrette.
Push a little of the reserved egg yolk through a
fine strainer onto each mousse. Top with an
asparagus tip.

SERVES 4

Ogen Melon with Cheese Mousse and Raspberries

MELON DE LA TERRE SAINTE EN PARADE

One of the most refreshing and delicious drinks I have ever tasted was a simple fruit cocktail of the pulp of an Ogen melon, blended with a dash of dry vermouth or gin. Served in a tall glass with a few raspberries floating on top, it could lift the spirits on even the most dreary of days.

The following dish, with its balance of scented melon, fruity raspberries, and light, creamy cheese, is equally appealing. It is given here as an appetizer, but it also makes a splendid light summer lunch, especially for those watching their weight.

2 medium Ogen melons
6 oz. (185 g) low-fat soft cheese
1 egg, hard-boiled and chopped
1 teaspoon dry vermouth
pinch of cayenne pepper
2 cups (8 oz., 250 g) fresh raspberries

Halve the melons and discard the seeds. Use a melon baller to scoop small balls of fruit out of the melons. Set aside the melon balls.

Mash together the cheese and egg. Pass through a strainer or sieve if necessary to obtain a well-blended mixture. Stir in the vermouth and season with a little cayenne. Shape into balls the same size as the melon pieces.

Wash and drain the raspberries. Arrange an equal amount of melon, cheese, and raspberries on 4 individual plates or in 4 small bowls. No dressing is needed. Decorate with a sprig or two of apple mint, then serve.

SERVES 4

Mango Appetizer from Martinique

SOUSCAILLE

Fresh mango is becoming increasingly popular as the basis for a light meal, especially with salads or fish. In this dish it stands all by itself, with just a piquant dressing to bring out the natural flavors.

2 large green mangoes, peeled and thinly sliced

DRESSING
2/3 cup (5 fl. oz., 155 ml) tomato juice
2 garlic cloves, chopped
1 green sweet pepper (capsicum), seeded and chopped
juice of 1 lime
1 tablespoon clear honey
sea salt and freshly ground black pepper

Put the mango slices in a shallow bowl. Place the tomato juice, garlic, sweet pepper, and lime juice in a blender or food processor and reduce to a smooth purée. Season to taste with honey, salt, and pepper.

Pour the sauce over the mango slices and leave to marinate for at least 20 minutes.

Serve the mango slices on individual plates. Sprigs of fresh coriander make a pleasant garnish. Thinly sliced whole-wheat (wholemeal) bread, lightly buttered, can be offered as well.

SERVES 4

Pictured opposite: Ogen Melon with Cheese Mousse and Raspberries

Hot Entrées

Les Petites Entrées Chaudes

TOMATOES STUFFED WITH GOAT'S CHEESE, NUTS, AND GARLIC

....

TOMATES RIVIÉRA

Baked stuffed tomatoes have a tendency to be insipid, but a rich and flavorsome filling ensures that this is not the case here.

4 large tomatoes
1/2 cup (2 oz., 60 g) chopped walnuts
1/2 cup (1 oz., 30 g) soft whole-wheat
(wholemeal) breadcrumbs
2 cloves garlic, crushed
2 oz. (60 g) goat's cheese
1 tablespoon chopped fresh herbs
1 egg, beaten
sea salt and freshly ground black pepper

Trim the stems of the tomatoes, turn upside-down, and cut one-third off the base of each.
Scoop out all the pulp, discarding the seeds where possible. Chop the flesh to make a pulp and set aside. Place the tomato shells hole-down to drain while the filling is being prepared.

Put the walnuts, breadcrumbs, and garlic in a bowl, then mash together with the cheese. Add the herbs and stir in the egg. Stir in the tomato pulp and ensure that everything is well mixed. Season to taste.

Fill the tomato shells with the mixture and stand in a shallow baking pan. Bake in a preheated oven at 450°F (230°C) for 5 to 8 minutes, so that the filling is cooked but the tomatoes have not had time to split or collapse. Serve at once.

SERVES 4

Pictured on previous pages: Tomatoes Stuffed with Goat's Cheese, Nuts, and Garlic
Pictured opposite: Mushrooms in a Creamy Mustard Sauce

MUSHROOMS IN A CREAMY MUSTARD SAUCE

....

CHAMPIGNONS DE PARIS À LA MOUTARDE

In the days before Les Halles was a fashionable shopping center, it was the central vegetable market for all Paris. The tiny white mushrooms that were sold there, still fresh with dew from the fields, are always known in France as 'champignons de Paris'. Now they are frequently cultivated indoors.

1 lb. (500 g) small button mushrooms (ideally, all the same size), cleaned and ends trimmed
juice of 1 lemon
2 tablespoons brandy
1/4 cup (2 fl. oz., 60 ml) sunflower oil
1 small shallot, chopped
2 tablespoons sour cream
2 tablespoons tomato paste (purée)
2 teaspoons honey
sea salt and freshly ground black pepper
small pinch of cayenne pepper
2 tablespoons Dijon mustard
1 tablespoon soft whole-wheat
(wholemeal) breadcrumbs
2 tablespoons grated cheese

Put the mushrooms in a bowl and stir in the lemon juice and brandy. Leave to marinate for 10 minutes.

Heat the oil in a skillet or frying pan and sauté the shallot for 1 minute without browning. Pour in the marinade juices and cook for 2 minutes to reduce liquid.

Add the mushrooms and cook for a further 2 minutes. Remove them from the skillet with a slotted spoon and keep warm in a shallow ovenproof dish.

Stir the sour cream, tomato paste, honey, salt, pepper and cayenne into the skillet juices and boil for 2 minutes to reduce further. Last, stir in the mustard but do not allow the sauce to boil.

Pour the sauce over the mushrooms. Combine the breadcrumbs and cheese, and sprinkle over the mushrooms. Brown under a broiler (griller) until golden. Serve with triangles of toasted whole-wheat (wholemeal) bread.

SERVES 4

WARM SALAD OF MUSHROOMS ON MANDARIN ORANGES AND CURLY ENDIVE

LA SALADE MARY CONIL

Anyone who can put up with me for forty-five years deserves a special award for bravery and fortitude. I have always been a difficult, cantankerous and exacting man, and no one knows this better than my dear wife Mary. Many young apprentices, who have since become top chefs, remember me as a demanding teacher — but they learned their skills well. Still, it is my wife who has stayed by my side over the years, and I pay tribute to her now with a dish she herself is responsible for.
It is based upon an inspired creation of hers, made when unexpected guests arrived one day, and proves that we have more than one chef in the Conil household.

2 oz. (60 g) butter
4 shallots, chopped
1 lb. (500 g) mushrooms, sliced
sea salt and freshly ground black pepper
1/2 cup (4 fl. oz., 125 ml) heavy cream
4 eggs, beaten
juice of 1 lemon
1 cup (2 oz., 60 g) fresh brioche crumbs
1 head curly endive
2 mandarin oranges (tangerines), segmented
1/2 cup (2 oz., 60 g) shelled pistachio nuts
fresh tarragon, chopped, to garnish

Melt the butter in a saucepan and sauté the shallots until tender. Stir in the mushrooms, cover, and simmer for about 3 minutes. Season with salt and pepper, and allow to cool.

In a bowl, beat together the cream, eggs, and lemon juice. Stir in the mushrooms, then beat in the brioche crumbs. Check the seasoning.

Spoon the mixture into 6 greased ramekins, then place these in a water bath or bain marie. Bake in a preheated oven at 400°F (200°C) for 25 minutes. Remove from the oven and leave to cool.

While the mushroom custards are cooling, wash and drain the curly endive and separate the leaves. Place on individual plates and sprinkle with mandarin orange segments and pistachio nuts.

Turn the warm custards out on the salad. Sprinkle with tarragon and serve while still warm.

VARIATIONS
The salad leaves and nuts can be varied endlessly. Fresh breadcrumbs can take the place of brioche crumbs. Garnish the salad with edible flower petals instead of tarragon.

SERVES 6

CARROT AND BROCCOLI SOUFFLÉS

PETITS SOUFFLÉS DE CAROTTE ET BROCCOLI

Here is the opportunity to attempt a soufflé with every chance of success, even if you have never dared to before!

2 oz. (60 g) butter, softened
1/2 cup (2 oz., 60 g) crushed salted peanuts

SOUFFLÉ
2 tablespoons (1 oz., 30 g) butter
2 tablespoons chopped onion
1 1/2 cups (3 oz., 90 g) soft whole-wheat (wholemeal) breadcrumbs
3 oz. (90 g) cooked, puréed carrot
3 oz. (90 g) cooked, puréed broccoli
3 oz. (90 g) cream cheese
1 egg, beaten
3 egg yolks
sea salt and freshly ground black pepper
pinch each of grated nutmeg and ground ginger
5 egg whites

Coat the sides of 6 individual soufflé dishes with a thick layer of butter. Sprinkle in the crushed peanuts so they stick to the sides.

To make the soufflé, melt the butter in a saucepan. Stir-fry the onion for 1 minute. Add the breadcrumbs, the two purées (drained of excess liquid), and the cream cheese. Beat the mixture until thoroughly blended. Stir in the beaten whole egg and the 3 egg yolks. Heat gently and thoroughly, but do not allow to bubble. Remove from heat and cool for 10 minutes. Season with salt, pepper, nutmeg, and ginger. Transfer to a bowl.

In another bowl, beat the egg whites with a pinch of salt until stiff. Add half the egg white to the vegetable mixture and mix well. Stir the remainder in very gently and lightly.

Fill each soufflé dish to the brim with the mixture. Then, with the back of a teaspoon, make a channel around the top to separate the soufflé from the edge of the dish by at least 1/4 in. (6 mm) wide and deep. With a fork, mark the top of the soufflé in a criss-cross pattern.

Put on a baking tray in the center of an oven preheated at 400°F (200°C) and cook for 16 to 22 minutes. Do not open the oven during this time.

Serve immediately, in the soufflé dishes.

SERVES 6

Pictured right: Sautéed Lentil Cromesquis

SAUTÉED LENTIL CROMESQUIS

CROMESQUIS DE LENTILLES

There is a distinction between a cromesqui and a croquette of which most people are unaware, partly because the former is untranslatable and partly because the two terms are used interchangeably. Strictly speaking, a cromesqui is coated in batter and shallow-fried, while a croquette is rolled in breadcrumbs and deep-fried.

In this recipe I have created a delicious blend of green lentils, puréed vegetables, and hard-boiled eggs, shaped into a cylinder, rolled in flour, beaten egg, and breadcrumbs, then sautéed in olive oil. Other pulses could be substituted for the lentils.

1 cup (6½ oz., 200 g) green lentils, picked over

5 cups (2 imp. pints, 1.25 litres) water

4 oz. (125 g) potatoes, sliced

4 oz. (125 g) carrots, chopped

4 oz. (125 g) onions, chopped

1 garlic clove, chopped

1 sprig thyme

2 eggs, hard-boiled and chopped

2 eggs, beaten

sea salt and freshly ground black pepper

2 oz. (60 g) butter

whole-wheat (wholemeal) flour, for batter

extra 2 eggs, beaten, for batter

2 cups dried breadcrumbs, for coating

vegetable oil (preferably olive), for frying

Wash the lentils, soak in water to cover for 3 to 6 hours, then drain.

In the 5 cups of water, boil the lentils, potatoes, carrots, onions, garlic, and thyme for 45 minutes. Drain. Remove the thyme. Blend the lentils and vegetables to a purée.

Combine the purée with the hard-boiled and the beaten eggs. Season lightly with salt and pepper, and stir in the butter.

Divide the mixture into 16 equal parts. Roll each in flour and shape into cylinders. Coat in the additional beaten egg and then the breadcrumbs.

Heat the oil in a large skillet or frying pan and shallow-fry the cromesquis for 3 minutes, until golden brown all over. Drain and serve with a tomato salad, or by themselves as a snack.

SERVES 4

Eggplant Topped with Gruyère Cheese

Aubergine au Gruyère

This is a favorite hot starter. Gruyère can be substituted by any cheese with good melting qualities, such as Cheddar, Gouda, double Gloucester, Port Salut, or Cantal. You can experiment to find the one you like best. For reasons of health, I am inclined to use soybean or sunflower oils in fried dishes, but this dish really benefits from the special flavor of olive oil, the favorite of the French. If it is heated to the correct temperature (375°F (190°C)) before you start frying, the eggplants (aubergines) will cook before they have a chance to absorb too much oil. If you have no thermometer, drop a cube of bread into the oil — if it is golden brown within 10 seconds, the oil is hot enough. However, try not to let it get too hot, to smoking point, as this affects flavor and the eggplant may burn. Never overfill your french fryer or deep fryer, and do not fry too much at once. It is better to cook in small batches, otherwise the temperature of the oil will drop and the food will be oily and unpleasant. Allow the oil to reheat between batches, too.

2 large eggplants (aubergines)
sea salt
1 cup (4 oz., 125 g) whole-wheat (wholemeal) flour,
seasoned with sea salt and freshly ground black pepper
1 garlic clove, finely crushed
5 cups (2 imp. pints, 1.25 litres) olive oil
8 oz. (250 g) Gruyère cheese, thinly sliced

Cut the eggplants lengthwise into slices ¼ in. (6 mm) thick. Sprinkle each slice with salt and leave to exude its bitter juices for 25 minutes. Wash, drain, and dry thoroughly.

Mix the seasoned flour with the garlic and coat each eggplant slice, shaking off any excess.

Heat the oil and deep fry each eggplant slice for 1 minute. Drain on paper towels.

Arrange the slices in a single layer on a flat baking sheet (tray) and place a slice of cheese over each one. Grill until the cheese is golden and serve at once.

Variations

Place on toasted bread for a snack meal.

Mozzarella is an excellent cheese to use in this dish, especially when sandwiched with the eggplant between two slices of hot toast in a variation of the famous French *Croque Monsieur*.

SERVES 4

Pictured opposite: Eggplant Topped with Gruyère Cheese

Exotic Crêpe Rolls

Épigrammes de Riz Elysée

Rice must be eaten with pulses or seeds, or both, to supply the body with proper nourishment. This dish provides additional protein in the form of eggs. I find that American rice, from Carolina in particular, is the best for the pilaf-style cooking that this recipe requires, but any patna rice with long slender grains will do.

⅓ cup (2 oz., 60 g) sweetcorn kernels
⅓ cup (2 oz., 60 g) fresh green peas
½ cup (4 fl. oz., 125 ml) peanut oil
1 medium onion, chopped
1 red sweet pepper (capsicum), deseeded and chopped
1 garlic clove, chopped
½ cup (4 oz., 125 g) brown rice
2 cups (16 fl. oz., 500 ml) water
1 teaspoon turmeric
sea salt and freshly ground black pepper
2 eggs, beaten
⅓ cup (2 oz., 60 g) diced dried figs
1½ quantities crêpe batter (see p. 152)

whole-wheat (wholemeal) flour, for dusting
vegetable oil, for frying

Boil the sweetcorn and peas for 5 minutes and set aside to cool. Heat the peanut oil in a large saucepan and stir-fry the onion until transparent. Add the sweet pepper and garlic, and cook for a further 2 minutes. Stir in the rice, making sure it is well impregnated with oil. Add the water and turmeric, and stir well. Transfer to a shallow earthenware dish and bake in a preheated oven at 400°F (200°C) for 45 minutes. Add the sweetcorn and peas, and salt and pepper to taste, 5 minutes before the end of the cooking time.

Remove from the oven and mix in the eggs to bind to a semisolid paste. Add the diced figs and adjust seasoning if necessary. Allow to cool.

Make 6 crêpes, 8 in. (20 cm) in diameter.

When the mixture is cold, lay the crêpes out flat and drop spoonfuls of the mixture onto each one, taking care to use equal amounts. Fold each crêpe around the mixture like an envelope to form neat elongated rolls. Make sure the filling is securely wrapped. Roll the crêpes in flour. Heat the oil in a skillet or frying pan and sauté the rolls until golden all over. Serve with a salad of bean sprouts in a vinaigrette sauce.

SERVES 6

THREE-LAYER VEGETABLE LOAF

CASSATE DE LÉGUMES ORLÉANAISE

The region where Joan of Arc came from has a rich repertoire of vegetable terrines such as this one, which is as good to eat as it is to look at.

1½ lbs. (750 g) carrots, sliced

1½ lbs. (750 g) green or string beans, ends removed

1½ lbs. (750 g) leeks, washed, trimmed, and sliced in 1-in. (2.5-cm) chunks

8 fresh tarragon leaves

8 chives, snipped

1 tablespoon chopped coriander leaves

1 teaspoon caraway seeds

8 oz. (250 g) cream cheese

6 eggs

sea salt and freshly ground black pepper

pinch of grated nutmeg

Cook the carrots, beans, and leeks separately for 15 minutes each. Drain well.

In a blender or food processor, purée the carrots with the tarragon, then set aside in a bowl. Purée the beans with the chives and set aside in another bowl. Purée the leeks with the coriander and caraway seeds and place in a third bowl.

Beat one-third of the cheese into each mixture, then add 2 beaten eggs to each. Mix well. Season to taste.

Grease a large loaf pan. Place the leek purée in the base of the pan, then the carrot purée, and top with the bean purée. Place in a water bath or bain marie and bake in a preheated oven at 400°F (200°C) for about 1¼ hours.

Remove from the oven and leave for 10 minutes. Unmold onto a warmed platter. Garnish with baby carrots flavored with honey and ginger.

VARIATION

The dish can be cooked in individual ramekins at the same temperature but for half the time.

SERVES 8

FRIED CORNMEAL GALETTES WITH SPICY RED SAUCE

GALETTE DE MAÏS, SAUCE ROUGEOLE

Corn, or maize, is grown all over France. It was once primarily food for cattle and chickens, and what little was eaten by humans was used to make traditional peasant dishes, variations of which can be found in most developing countries and in the Italian polenta. For a complete protein balance, corn must be eaten with a pulse or nuts or seeds. In this recipe, I have drawn on the peasant tradition, but added cheese and eggs for extra protein. These galettes could also be served with a green salad sprinkled with seeds or chopped nuts to complement the grain.

CORNMEAL GALETTES
5 cups (2 imp. pints, 1.25 litres) water
1½ cups (8 oz., 250 g) coarse cornmeal
2 oz. (60 g) butter
sea salt and freshly ground black pepper
3 eggs, beaten
whole-wheat (wholemeal) flour

extra butter, for frying
1 quantity Spicy Red Sauce (see p. 170)
1 cup (4 oz., 125 g) grated hard cheese

Boil the water in a saucepan and sprinkle in the cornmeal. Stir with a wooden spoon and cook gently for 25 to 35 minutes. Add butter, salt, and pepper. Remove from the heat and stir in the eggs.

Reheat and stir for 4 minutes. Pour into a greased jelly roll pan (Swiss roll tin) to a depth of ¾ in. (2 cm). Allow to cool.

When the cornmeal is cold and set, cut into small rounds about 2 in. (5 cm) in diameter. Coat the rounds in flour and sauté in butter for about 4 minutes, until golden on both sides. Keep warm on a serving platter while making the sauce.

Pour the sauce over the cornmeal galettes.

Serve with the grated cheese passed around separately, or sprinkled over the galettes and browned lightly under the broiler (griller).

SERVES 6

STUFFED ZUCCHINI

COURGETTES FARÇIES AUX MOUSSERONS

Mousserons à la Crème is a traditional Burgundian dish, a variation of which is used here as a filling for tender-crisp zucchini (courgettes).

4 large zucchini (courgettes)
2 oz. (60 g) butter
1 shallot, chopped
2 cloves garlic, crushed
1 cup (4 oz., 125 g) chopped button mushrooms
½ cup (4 oz., 125 g) cooked, drained, and chopped spinach
4 oz. (125 g) cream cheese
1 tablespoon tomato paste (purée)
sea salt and freshly ground black pepper
1 teaspoon honey
1 egg, beaten
½ cup (2 oz., 60 g) chopped pistachio nuts

Trim the ends of the zucchini, halve them lengthwise, and scoop out some of the flesh to form hollow 'boats'.

Bring a large pan of salted water to the boil and blanch the zucchini for 2 minutes. Drain well, then place in a greased earthenware dish.

Heat the butter in a saucepan and sauté the shallot and garlic for 2 minutes. Add the mushrooms and spinach, and cook gently for 4 minutes to remove any liquid.

Stir in the cream cheese, then the tomato paste. Season to taste with salt and pepper. Then stir in the honey.

Remove the saucepan from the heat and combine the egg and nuts with the spinach and cream cheese mixture.

Fill the zucchini halves with this mixture. Place the dish in a preheated oven at 400°F (200°C) for 5 minutes to heat. Serve hot, with a salad of thinly sliced tomatoes and perhaps a dressing of plain yogurt and watercress.

SERVES 4

Pictured above left: Three-layer Vegetable Loaf

MUSHROOM CAPS STUFFED WITH BRIE ON WHOLE-WHEAT CROUTONS

....

CHAMPIGNONS FARÇIE AU BRIE

This is an ideal hot starter, and one which my customers are delighted with whenever it appears on my menus. The general tendency is to overcook mushrooms and thus lose much of their wonderful earthy flavor. Here they are cooked just long enough to bring out their best. The large field mushrooms are ideal for this dish, particularly the French variety known as 'cèpes'.

4 large field mushrooms, washed and dried
thoroughly, stalks separated
1 garlic clove, chopped
1 small onion, chopped
1/2 cup (2 oz., 60 g) walnuts, chopped finely
2 oz. (60 g) good-quality butter, softened
2 oz. (60 g) mature Brie cheese
sea salt and freshly ground black pepper
pinch of mace
1 tablespoon each fresh chopped parsley and tarragon
1 egg, beaten
1 cup (2 oz., 60 g) soft whole-wheat
(wholemeal) breadcrumbs
4 slices whole-wheat (wholemeal) bread, cut into
squares slightly larger than mushrooms

Finely chop the mushroom stalks and mix with the garlic, onion, and walnuts.

Cream the butter and Brie together. Blend into the mushroom mixture with the salt, pepper, mace, parsley, and tarragon. Gradually add the egg and breadcrumbs to form a manageable, smooth paste.

Lightly grease an ovenproof dish and arrange the mushroom caps on it. Divide the paste into four balls and place one on each upturned cap.

Bake in a preheated oven at 400°F (200°C), or place under a hot broiler (griller). Cook for 10 minutes or until the filling is golden.

While the mushrooms are cooking, either fry or broil (grill) the bread to make croutons. Serve the mushrooms on these.

SERVES 4

Pictured opposite: Mushroom Caps Stuffed with Brie on Whole-Wheat Croutons, and Sweet Peppers Stuffed with Saffron Rice

SWEET PEPPERS STUFFED WITH SAFFRON RICE

....

POIVRON AU RIZ SAFFRANÉ

It is easy to get confused by all the names, types and colors of peppers. Like tomatoes, the color of peppers, or capsicums, as they are also known, changes with their stages of ripeness, from green to yellow to red. Their flavor changes, too, becoming sweeter as the fruit matures. Many cooks recommend skinning peppers before use by broiling (grilling) them until the skin can be peeled away. I prefer to leave the skin on.

1/2 cup (4 fl. oz., 125 ml) olive oil
1 green sweet pepper (capsicum), deseeded and cubed
1 medium onion, chopped
1 stalk fennel, chopped
2 cloves garlic, chopped
1/2 cup (4 oz., 125 g) brown rice
1 1/2 cups (12 fl. oz., 375 ml) water
2 tablespoons tomato paste (purée)
1 cup (4 oz., 125 g) chopped fresh spinach *or* sorrel leaves
large pinch of saffron *or* turmeric
1/3 cup (2 oz., 60 g) green peas
sea salt and freshly ground black pepper
4 red sweet peppers (capsicums), tops sliced off and
seeds and white membranes removed

Heat the oil in a saucepan and stir-fry green sweet pepper, onion, fennel, and garlic for 4 minutes. Do not brown.

Add the rice and stir well. Stir in the water. Add the tomato paste, spinach or sorrel, spice, and peas. Bring to the boil, cover, and cook for 30 to 40 minutes or until the rice is cooked but still firm and has absorbed all the water. Add more water during cooking if it is absorbed too quickly. Season to taste with salt and pepper.

Fill the red sweet peppers with the rice mixture.

Place the peppers, upright, in a shallow baking pan. Add water to half-way up the peppers. Season the water and cover the dish with aluminum foil.

Braise in a preheated oven at 400°F (200°C) for about 35 minutes.

Flavor the cooking water, if necessary, with a little yeast extract to form a stock. Serve the peppers hot or cold, moistened with a little stock.

VARIATION

For a more substantial dish, add diced hard-boiled eggs, nuts, cooked beans, grated cheese or diced mushrooms, to the cooked rice mixture.

SERVES 4

CHESTNUT TARTLETS

LES DORINES AUX MARRONS

This delicate tartlet belongs to the Auvergne region, where chestnuts abound. It is usually served as a dessert, flavored with plenty of sugar, but I have chosen to omit this in favor of a savory dish, which I feel brings out the mellow taste of the chestnuts to pleasing effect.

PASTRY
3 oz. (90 g) margarine
1 egg yolk
1½ cups (6 oz., 185 g) whole-wheat (wholemeal) flour
sea salt
1 tablespoon water

CUSTARD
1⅓ cup (11 fl. oz., 340 ml) milk
3 egg yolks
1 tablespoon cornmeal
sea salt
pinch of grated nutmeg

FILLING
1 cup (6 oz., 185 g) chestnut paste (purée)
2 tablespoons curd cheese
1 garlic clove, crushed, *or* 1 tablespoon snipped chives
pinch of grated nutmeg

Prepare the pastry by creaming together the margarine and egg yolk in a bowl. Gradually stir in the flour and salt to form a stiff dough, then add water to achieve the correct consistency for pastry. Cover and refrigerate for 30 minutes.

Meanwhile, prepare the custard. Bring the milk to the boil in a saucepan. In a bowl, beat the egg yolks with the cornmeal, salt, and nutmeg, then gradually add the hot milk, stirring constantly to achieve a smooth paste. Return the mixture to the saucepan and heat gently for 2 minutes to thicken the custard. Cool.

Beat together the chestnut paste (purée), cheese, garlic or chives, and nutmeg.

Divide the dough into 8 equal pieces. Roll out each and line greased individual tartlet pans.

Half-fill the pastry bases with chestnut mixture. Top each with the custard.

Bake the tartlets in a preheated oven at 400°F (200°C) for 20 to 25 minutes, until risen and golden. Serve hot or cold.

SERVES 8

Pictured above right: Spinach and Cheese Roulade

FRESH ASPARAGUS IN A PASTRY CASE WITH TARRAGON SAUCE

LA TOURTE D'ASPERGE BÉARNAISE

For this recipe, I have modified the true béarnaise sauce to suit my little asparagus tartlets. Because the tarts are baked in the oven, the sauce has to be stabilized with flour.

SAUCE
2 tablespoons (1 oz., 30 g) butter
¼ cup (1 oz., 30 g) whole-wheat (wholemeal) flour
1¾ cups (10 fl. oz., 310 ml) milk
sea salt and freshly ground black pepper
pinch of grated nutmeg
2 egg yolks
2 eggs, beaten
½ cup (2 oz., 60 g) grated Gruyère or Cheddar cheese
1 tablespoon each chopped fresh parsley and tarragon
juice of 1 lemon

16 asparagus stalks
1 quantity shortcrust pastry (see p. 158)

To make the sauce, melt the butter in a saucepan. Add the flour and cook without browning for 1 minute. Pour the milk in gradually, stirring to avoid lumps. Boil gently for 5 minutes. Season with salt, pepper, and nutmeg.

Take off the heat. Add the egg yolks and beaten egg, grated cheese, and herbs. Cool the sauce completely before adding the lemon juice.

Meanwhile, prepare the asparagus for cooking: scrape the stem of each, avoiding any damage to the tip. Wash well and cut off the woody end of the stem. Tie into two bundles with string.

Boil in salted water for 12 to 15 minutes. Lift out of the water and refresh in a bowl of cold water. Drain well. Cut each asparagus stalk in two, so that the stems and tips are separated.

Lightly grease a 10-in. (25-cm) quiche pan.

Dust a board with flour and roll out the pastry into a circle 14 in. (35 cm) in diameter and ¼ in. (6 mm) thick. Line the quiche pan with the pastry. Trim any surplus, then press gently round the edges to make the sides and border neat and even. Crimp the edges by pinching. Brush the bottom of the pastry base with melted butter and arrange the asparagus over it in a pattern, with the stems at the bottom and the tips on top. Cover with the cold sauce. Bake in a preheated oven at 400°F (200°C) for 30 minutes, until the pastry is thoroughly cooked. Serve hot or cold.

SERVES 4

SPINACH AND CHEESE ROULADE

....

ROULADE D'ÉPINARDS

A roulade may appear a little involved at first, but the result of this classic French technique makes the effort well worthwhile.

6 eggs, separated
1/2 cup (2 oz., 60 g) whole-wheat (wholemeal) flour
5 oz. (155 g) cooked, puréed spinach, squeezed dry
1 garlic clove, finely chopped
sea salt and freshly ground black pepper
olive oil, for greasing
1 1/2 cups (6 oz., 185 g) grated Gruyère cheese
1 oz. (30 g) butter, melted
watercress *or* other green herb, to garnish

Separate the eggs. In a bowl, combine the egg yolks with the flour, spinach, garlic, salt, and pepper to form a smooth mixture. In a separate bowl, beat the egg whites with a pinch of salt until stiff. Fold into the spinach mixture.

Line a jelly roll cake pan (Swiss roll tin) with parchment or baking paper and grease thoroughly. Spread the mixture evenly onto the parchment paper to form a rectangle about 12 in. x 9 in. (30 cm x 22.5 cm).

Bake in a preheated oven at 400°F (200°C) for 15 minutes until risen and lightly browned.

Lay a clean cloth on a smooth surface. Cover with a sheet of waxed paper. Carefully turn the pan over onto the paper. Remove the pan and peel off the parchment paper. Sprinkle the spinach sponge with two-thirds of the Gruyère cheese.

Lift the cloth at the short side of the sponge and roll the sponge up on itself, pulling the paper and the cloth away from the sponge as you go. Wrap the rolled sponge tightly in the cloth for 5 minutes, then remove the cloth.

Place the rolled sponge on an oiled baking sheet (tray). Brush the top with the butter and sprinkle with the remaining cheese. Return the roulade to the oven for a further 5 minutes or until the cheese on top is lightly browned.

Serve the roulade, cut into thick slices, with a garnish of watercress or other green herb.

SERVES 4

BAKED SPINACH TIMBALES

TIMBALES D'ÉPINARD VIROFLAY

This dish is named after the town of Viroflay in Île de France, once famous for its spinach.

2 lbs. (1 kg) fresh spinach, washed and coarse stems discarded
4 oz. (125 g) butter
1 cup (2 oz., 60 g) soft whole-wheat (wholemeal) breadcrumbs
1¼ cups (10 fl. oz., 310 ml) light cream
3 eggs, beaten
sea salt and freshly ground black pepper
pinch of grated nutmeg
4 tomatoes, skinned and sliced, to garnish

LEMON SAUCE
½ cup (4 fl. oz., 125 ml) plain yogurt
juice and grated rind of ¼ lemon
1 garlic clove
sea salt and freshly ground black pepper
1 teaspoon honey

Select 16 large, undamaged spinach leaves. Boil for 2 minutes. Refresh in cold water, then drain.

Use half the butter to generously coat 4 dariole molds. Line with the cooked spinach leaves.

Boil the remaining spinach for 6 minutes. Drain, refresh in cold water, and drain again. Squeeze dry, then chop finely.

Melt the remaining butter in a saucepan. Add the chopped spinach and heat until all the butter is absorbed. Add the breadcrumbs and cream. Remove from the heat and stir in the beaten eggs. Season with salt, pepper, and nutmeg.

Fill the lined molds with this mixture and cover with buttered aluminum foil. Place the molds in a water bath or bain marie. Bake in a preheated oven at 350°F (180°C) for 45 to 50 minutes or until the mixture is set and firm.

While the molds are cooking, blend all the sauce ingredients in a blender or food processor.

Remove the molds from the water bath. Cool for 12 minutes, then turn out onto a serving dish. Decorate each mold with a slice of tomato. Serve with the sauce on the side.

VARIATIONS
A hot béchamel sauce, flavored with a little lemon, goes well with this dish, as does a simple tomato sauce or a cheese sauce. The mold can also be garnished with croutons. Lettuce or chard leaves can be used as a substitute for spinach.

SERVES 4

PARISIAN RICE CASTLES

TIMBALES DE RIZ PARISIENNE

½ cup (3 oz., 90 g) short-grain rice
2½ cups (1 imp. pint, 625 ml) milk
sea salt and freshly ground black pepper
grated nutmeg
½ cup (4 fl. oz., 125 ml) light cream
3 eggs, lightly beaten
1 cup (4 oz., 125 g) white button mushrooms, thinly sliced

Put the rice in a large, shallow pie plate. Heat the milk and pour over the rice. Bake uncovered in a preheated oven at 350°F (180°C) for 40 minutes or until the rice has absorbed the milk almost completely. Cool, season to taste with salt, pepper, and nutmeg, then allow to become completely cold.

Meanwhile, increase the oven temperature to 400°F (200°C).

In a bowl, combine the cream, eggs, and rice mixture. Add the mushrooms. Check seasoning.

Grease 6 metal dariole molds and fill with the mixture. Place the molds in a water bath or bain marie. Bake in the oven for a further 15 minutes.

Remove from the oven and turn out the timbales onto individual serving plates. Serve with a few lightly dressed salad leaves.

SERVES 6

Pictured opposite: Baked Spinach Timbales

Hot and Chilled Soups
Les Potages Chauds et Froids

PUMPKIN SOUP

LA SOUPE AU POTIRON

Pumpkin soup is becoming increasingly popular around the world, but some people still do not know quite what to do with this attractive-looking vegetable. There are, of course, many uses for it — in soups, stews, and desserts such as the famous American Pumpkin Pie. Provençal dishes combine pumpkin with herbs and garlic, rice or pasta to make delicious and filling meals, and home-brewers may be interested to know that an excellent cordial can be made from it.

The pumpkin's bright orange flesh gives this soup an attractive appearance, which particularly appeals to children, and the flavor will be appreciated by everyone, even gourmets. It was my favorite soup as a child, and this recipe of my grandmother Mathilde's is still the best I have found.

4 oz. (125 g) butter

1 large onion, thinly sliced

1 lb. (500 g) pumpkin flesh, thinly sliced

8 oz. (250 g) potatoes, thinly sliced

5 cups (2 imp. pints, 1.25 litres) water

1 cup (8 fl. oz., 250 ml) sour cream

sea salt and freshly ground black pepper

pinch of ground ginger

whole-wheat (wholemeal) bread, cut into sippets and fried, *or* crackers

Heat the butter in a large saucepan and sauté the onion until transparent — this takes about 4 minutes.

Add the pumpkin and potatoes and cook gently for a further 4 minutes.

Stir in the water and boil for 30 minutes, until the vegetables are soft. Pass the soup through a Mouli grater or strainer.

Reheat, stir in the sour cream, then season with salt, pepper, and ginger.

Serve with fried bread or crackers.

SERVES 6-8

Pictured on previous pages: Pumpkin Soup
Pictured right: Beet Soup with Red Wine

RIVIERA SOUP WITH GARLIC, SAFFRON, AND BASIL

LA BOUILLABAISSE DE LÉGUMES RIVIERA

Some people say that a bouillabaisse without fish is a contradiction in terms, but this one is a traditional French vegetable soup.

4 oz. (125 g) onions, thinly sliced

4 oz. (125 g) leeks, white part only, sliced

1 lb. (500 g) tomatoes, skinned, deseeded, and chopped

1 lb. (500 g) potatoes, diced

4 garlic cloves, chopped

1/2 cup (4 fl. oz., 125 ml) olive oil

1/4 cup (2 oz., 60 g) tomato paste (purée)

pinch each of thyme, celery seeds, and saffron

1 bay leaf

1 teaspoon chopped fresh basil

juice and finely grated rind of 1 orange

7 cups (3 imp. pints, 1.75 litres) water

2 tablespoons yeast extract

sea salt and freshly ground black pepper

LIAISON

3 egg yolks

1 garlic clove, crushed

2 tablespoons olive oil

3 tablespoons cornstarch (cornflour)

1/2 cup (4 fl. oz., 125 ml) water

1 teaspoon turmeric

pinch of chili powder (optional)

GARNISH

4 slices toasted whole-wheat (wholemeal) French bread, rubbed with garlic and cut into sippets

2 tablespoons fresh parsley leaves

Sauté all the vegetables in the oil in a large saucepan until soft — about 8 minutes.

Add the tomato paste, thyme, celery seeds, saffron, bay leaf, and the orange rind and juice. Stir in the water and yeast extract. Cook for 30 minutes.

Strain the soup and remove the bay leaf. Purée the vegetables in a blender or food processor with a little of the stock.

Return the purée and liquid to the pan and reheat.

In a bowl, combine the liaison ingredients. Add this mixture to the soup very slowly, stirring all the time. Boil for 5 minutes more.

Serve with a sprinkling of bread and parsley.

SERVES 12

BEET SOUP WITH RED WINE

LE DRAGON ROUGE

My family is descended from a small branch of the French aristocracy who lived in northern France until the French Revolution took many of their heads and all of their lands, but the family's recipes were a closely guarded secret. This soup is one of those recipes, an amalgam of French and Russian cuisine, named after the 'red dragon' of the Russian Revolution, but reminiscent of the splendor of earlier times.

2 lbs. (1 kg) beets (beetroot), washed

1¼ cups (10 fl. oz., 310 ml) red wine

large pinch of anise seed

½ cup (4 oz., 125 g) mixed butter and oil

1 medium onion, chopped

2 stalks celery, chopped

2 stalks fennel, chopped

2 carrots, peeled and sliced

4 oz. (125 g) cabbage, sliced

1 bouquet garni

5 cups (2 imp. pints, 1.25 litres) water

sea salt and freshly ground black pepper

pinch of Demerara (raw) sugar

⅔ cup (5 fl. oz., 155 ml) sour cream

croutons *or* slices of whole-wheat (wholemeal) bread

Boil half of the beets in salted water for 30 minutes. Peel and cut them into thin strips. Marinate in the red wine and anise seed for 1 hour.

Peel and slice the remaining beets.

Heat the butter and oil in a large pan. Sauté the raw beets, onion, celery, fennel, carrots, cabbage, and bouquet garni for 8 minutes. Add the water and boil for 30 minutes.

When the vegetables are tender, remove the bouquet garni and strain the soup. Purée the vegetables in a blender or food processor with just a little liquid.

Reheat the purée. Add the marinated beets and the wine, and season to taste with salt, pepper, and sugar. Lastly, stir in the sour cream, diluted with a little water if very thick.

Serve hot with croutons or bread. The soup can also be quite delicious served cold.

Note: Beets are best marinated in wine rather than in vinegar. The acid gives the soup its characteristic red color without the dominating sharpness of vinegar. Without the wine, the broth will be a golden-yellow.

SERVES 6-8

NORMANDY VEGETABLE SOUP

SOUPE NORMANDE AU CALVADOS

This thick and warming vegetable soup can be varied to use the best produce available in the store or the glut in your garden. The traditional Norman ingredient of cream is quite often replaced with tofu by modern vegetarian cooks in France, but it is worth retaining that other item of Normandy produce — Calvados — for a very special soup.

¼ cup (2 fl. oz., 60 ml) vegetable oil
1⅓ cups (8 oz., 250 g) diced potatoes
1 small bunch chives, snipped
8 oz. (250 g) sorrel, spinach, *or* lettuce leaves, torn and coarse stems discarded
1⅓ cups (8 oz., 250 g) runner beans, ends discarded, cut diagonally, *or* garden peas
3½ cups (28 fl. oz., 875 ml) boiling water
2 oz. (60 g) tofu
sea salt and freshly ground black pepper
6 slices whole-wheat (wholemeal) French bread
¼ cup (2 fl. oz., 60 ml) Calvados

Heat the oil in a large saucepan and sauté the potatoes and chives for 2 minutes. Add the torn leaves and cook for a further 2 minutes.

Stir in the water. Cover the saucepan and simmer for 35 minutes or until the potatoes are cooked. After about 20 minutes of cooking, add the peas and beans.

Add the tofu and purée briefly so that the soup has a thick, chunky texture. If you have an old-fashioned food mill, use it to give the texture that this soup requires.

Reheat the soup and season with salt and pepper to taste.

Place a slice of bread in each of six warmed soup bowls. Soak each slice with a little Calvados. Pour the soup over and serve at once.

VARIATION
Soy milk can be used instead of tofu, in which case, simply stir it in while reheating the soup. Traditionalists may, of course, use cream.

Note: If sorrel is not used, stir in the juice of half a lemon when reheating to provide acidity.

SERVES 6

Pictured opposite: Normandy Vegetable Soup, and Onion Soup with Madeira

ONION SOUP WITH MADEIRA

LA SOUPE À L'OIGNON DUCASTAING

In 1932 my father, Octave, bought a fashionable brasserie-restaurant in Paris, the Ducastaing. Escoffier himself patronized it, and this is how I had the opportunity to train as a chef, not only in our restaurant but in many others whose owners were friends of the family. One of the Ducastaing's great features was its onion soup. This was always cooked to order — never in advance. My father used to say that onion soup was ideal for hangovers. Most of our patrons gave themselves frequent opportunities to try this theory out!

4 oz. (125 g) butter *or* ½ cup (4 fl. oz., 125 g) oil
1 lb. (500 g) onions, thinly sliced
½ cup (2 oz., 60 g) whole-wheat (wholemeal) flour
½ cup (4 fl. oz., 125 ml) dry Madeira
10 cups (4 imp. pints, 2.5 litres) water *or* vegetable stock
1 cup (4 oz., 125 g) grated Gruyère cheese
1 tablespoon sea salt
freshly ground black pepper
large pinch of dried thyme
large pinch of ground mace
1 tablespoon yeast extract

GARNISH
1 cup (4 oz., 125 g) grated Gruyère cheese
1 egg yolk
2 tablespoons (1 oz., 30 g) butter
12 slices toasted whole-wheat (wholemeal) French bread

Heat the butter in a large saucepan. Sauté the onions until translucent (about 6 minutes), then allow them to turn slightly golden.

Sprinkle in the flour and stir well. Stir in the Madeira and water or stock. Boil for 20 minutes, then add the cheese, salt, pepper, thyme, mace, and yeast extract. Simmer for a further 5 minutes.

Meanwhile, prepare the garnish. Blend the cheese, egg yolk, and butter to a paste. Spread a little on each slice of toast and brown under the broiler (griller).

Serve the soup in individual tureens, floating one slice of cheesy toast on each bowl.

Note: If you have no Madeira, dry or medium sherry or white port will do, or even a dry white wine is good.

SERVES 12

CREAM OF SORREL SOUP

CRÈME D'OSEILLE

French sorrel (Rumex scutatus) has juicy, fleshy leaves that are acid-tasting due to their high oxalic acid content. Oxalic acid combines with calcium and magnesium in the body to form an insoluble salt, which renders these minerals unusable, and the calcium oxalate crystals must be passed out of the body in the urine. Foods containing oxalic acid also include beets (beetroot), rhubarb, spinach, and green tomatoes, so if you eat these foods in any quantity it is advisable to drink plenty of liquids with them to avoid developing kidney stones.

In France, sorrel is often used in the same way as spinach, in salads. Like spinach, it is high in iron and vitamin A, and French sorrel is lower in oxalic acid than common wild sorrel. One variation of this soup is to use half spinach and half sorrel.

2 oz. (60 g) butter
1/4 cup (2 fl. oz., 60 ml) vegetable oil
8 oz. (250 g) sorrel leaves, washed, drained, and cut into 2-in. (5-cm) pieces
4 oz. (125 g) leek, white part only, washed, drained, and cut into 2-in. (5-cm) pieces
4 oz. (125 g) potatoes, peeled and sliced
7 cups (3 imp. pints, 1.5 litres) water
4 egg yolks
1 tablespoon arrowroot
1/2 cup (4 fl. oz., 125 ml) light whipping cream
sea salt and freshly ground black pepper
freshly grated nutmeg
1 teaspoon Demerara (raw) sugar
whole-wheat (wholemeal) bread, cut into sippets and fried

Heat the butter and oil in a large saucepan. Add the sorrel, leeks, and potatoes, and cook gently for 5 minutes. Set aside ⅔ cup (155 ml, 5 fl. oz.) water. Add the rest of the water to the saucepan and boil for 20 minutes.

In a bowl, blend the egg yolks, arrowroot, and cream with the ⅔ cup of water. Stir this mixture into the soup to thicken. Cook the soup for a further 4 minutes, just boiling, until it is perfectly smooth in texture.

Season to taste with salt, pepper and nutmeg. Sprinkle in the sugar to counteract the acidity of the soup.

Serve with fried bread.

SERVES 6–8

Pictured above right: Asparagus Soup with Quail Eggs

MUSHROOM SOUP WITH EGGS AND CREAM

VELOUTÉ AUX CHAMPIGNONS

The problem when cooking mushrooms for soups and sauces is keeping them white. Cultured button mushrooms can be used, but they tend to be flavorless, and they must be blanched in lemon juice to retain their whiteness. Field mushrooms give a wonderful flavor, but turn black when cooked and discolor the dish. Nevertheless, you may find it worth the less attractive color to get a more richly flavored soup — it is certainly worth a try.

For this soup I have used white mushrooms, since this is an elegant dish whose appearance might be important to you. Their flavor can be enhanced, but not swamped, by the addition of other vegetables and herbs.

2 oz. (60 g) butter
1/4 cup (2 fl. oz., 60 ml) vegetable oil
1 lb. (500 g) white button mushrooms, trimmed of ends, washed, and dried
1 medium onion, chopped
1 small leek, cleaned and sliced
3 celery stalks, sliced
4 oz. (125 g) potatoes, peeled and sliced
5 cups (2 imp. pints, 1.25 litres) water
5 cups (2 imp. pints, 1.25 litres) milk
2 egg yolks
1/2 cup (4 fl. oz., 125 ml) heavy cream
2 tablespoons cornstarch (cornflour)
sea salt and freshly ground black pepper
pinch of ground mace
pinch of ground turmeric
pinch of celery seeds
1 garlic clove, crushed
juice and finely grated rind of 1 lemon

Heat the butter and oil together in a large saucepan and sauté all the vegetables for 8 minutes, covered with a lid but stirring now and then. Add the water and boil for 25 minutes.

Strain the liquid and return it to the saucepan. Blend the vegetables in a blender or food processor with a little of the liquid, then return to the pan. Add the milk.

Mix together the egg yolks, cream, and cornstarch in a bowl. Stir into the soup. Reheat and allow to boil for 5 minutes.

Season to taste with salt and pepper, and add the spices and garlic. Stir in the lemon juice and rind just before serving.

SERVES 12

Asparagus Soup with Quail Eggs

La Crème d'Asperge aux Oeufs de Cailles

The asparagus spear has been held in the highest esteem by gourmets since Ancient Greek and Roman times. It is raised from seed and grows best in very rich soil. The best French varieties are Lauris and Argenteuil, but there are many others, all varying in color, size, and taste. In the United States, the green variety is usual, while we French prefer the white shoots. The thinnest spears are known as 'grass'. Soups are usually made from the stalks of the plant, the tips being used for decoration or for serving with a hollandaise sauce or melted butter.

2 oz. (60 g) butter

1 small onion, sliced

1 stalk celery, sliced

1 lb. (500 g) green asparagus, stems scraped and cut into small pieces

5 cups (2 imp. pints, 1.25 litres) water

sea salt and freshly ground black pepper

3 egg yolks

1 cup (8 fl. oz., 250 ml) light *or* sour cream

2 tablespoons cornstarch (cornflour)

freshly grated nutmeg

juice and rind of 1 lemon (optional)

Garnish

12 fresh quail eggs

12 asparagus tips

Heat the butter in a saucepan and sauté the onion, celery, and asparagus for 4 minutes. Add the water and bring to the boil. Boil for 15 minutes.

Strain and set aside the liquid. Put the onion and asparagus into a blender with a little liquid. Blend to a purée. Transfer back to the saucepan along with the reserved liquid and reheat for 5 minutes. Season to taste with salt and pepper.

In a bowl, blend the egg yolks, cream, and cornstarch to a smooth mixture. Add 1 cup of the soup and stir well. Pour this into the saucepan of soup. Reheat to boiling point, adjust the seasoning and add the nutmeg to taste.

Boil the asparagus tips for 6 minutes in lightly salted water. Drain. Boil the quail eggs for 6 minutes, then remove shells.

If extra piquancy is desired, stir the lemon juice and rind into the soup just before serving. Serve the soup in individual bowls with 2 asparagus spears floating in each bowl, and 2 quail eggs either in the soup or served alongside.

Note: The quail eggs may be poached instead of hard-boiled, and served in the soup.

LEMONY VEGETABLE SOUP WITH CREAM

LA CITRONELLE

The richest lemon flavor is in the oil obtained from the fruit's skin — hence the need to use finely grated lemon rind in many dishes to obtain a true flavor. The herb citronella also has a subtle lemony flavor.
This soup uses lemon and citronella — though the latter can be replaced by the more common lemon mint, or even ordinary mint if necessary. It is a light and refreshing soup, good served hot or cold.

1/2 cup (4 fl. oz., 125 ml) vegetable oil
2/3 cup (4 oz., 125 g) chopped onion
2/3 cup (4 oz., 125 g) diced potatoes
2/3 cup (4 oz., 125 g) sliced leeks
2/3 cup (4 oz., 125 g) chopped celery
2/3 cup (4 oz., 125 g) diced fennel
2/3 cup (4 oz., 125 g) diced turnips
2/3 cup (4 oz., 125 g) shelled green peas
2/3 cup (4 oz., 125 g) diced rutabaga (swede)
1 cup (4 oz., 125 g) chopped spinach
3 quarts (5 imp. pints, 3 litres) water
sea salt and freshly ground black pepper
1 teaspoon Demerara (raw) sugar
1 teaspoon turmeric
4 leaves citronella *or* fresh mint, chopped
grated rind of 1 lemon
4 egg yolks
1/2 cup (4 fl. oz., 125 ml) light whipping cream
2 tablespoons cornstarch (cornflour)
extra 1/2 cup (4 fl. oz., 125 ml) water
juice of 1 lemon
1 1/4 cups (10 fl. oz., 310 ml) heavy cream (optional)
2 tablespoons cooked brown rice per serve (optional)

Heat the oil in a large pan. Sauté the vegetables for 8 minutes, covered with a lid. Add the water and boil for 30 minutes.

Put the vegetables in a blender or food processor with a little of the liquid and blend to a thin purée. Add more liquid if necessary.

Reheat the soup and stir in the salt, pepper, sugar, turmeric, herb, and grated lemon rind.

Combine the egg yolks, cream, cornstarch, and water in a bowl with a little of the soup. Pour this into the soup. Boil for 4 minutes to thicken. Stir in the lemon juice.

If the soup is to be served cold, stir the heavy cream in and chill before serving. If served hot, you could garnish each serve with brown rice.

SERVES 12–16

CHILLED LEEK AND POTATO SOUP

LA VICHYSSOISE

So much fuss is made about this simple soup, you would think it was some sort of culinary masterpiece. I even know of one chef who claims to have invented it! Yet Vichyssoise has been a favorite for as long as the leek has been used in soups. My grandmother was making it over fifty years ago. I remember we had it hot on the day it was made, then drank the rest of it cold the next day.

8 oz. (250 g) leeks, white part only, cleaned and sliced
4 oz. (125 g) potatoes, peeled and thinly sliced
4 oz. (125 g) butter
2 1/2 cups (1 imp. pint, 625 ml) water *or* vegetable stock
2 1/2 cups (1 imp. pint, 625 ml) milk
sea salt and freshly ground black pepper
1 teaspoon Demerara (raw) sugar
1/2 cup (4 fl. oz., 125 ml) heavy *or* sour cream (optional)
2 tablespoons chopped chives (optional)

Sauté the vegetables in the butter, without browning, for 4 minutes. Add the water or stock and boil for 20 minutes.

When the vegetables are tender, add the milk and heat for 5 minutes.

Blend to a thin purée in a blender or food processor. Reheat for 5 minutes. Season with salt, pepper, and sugar.

At this stage the soup could be served hot, with or without cream swirled in. If you wish to serve it cold, as is usual with Vichyssoise, chill the soup to below 40°F (5°C), then add the cream and sprinkle with chives before serving.

Note: The sugar enhances the flavor of the leek. The same effect can be achieved with monosodium glutamate. This is a natural substance which, while being tasteless on its own, brings out the flavor of other foods, just as salt and sugar do. Many bouillon (stock) cubes contain monosodium glutamate. However, some people have an allergic reaction to this substance, so you may prefer to avoid its use. Bouillon cubes or yeast extract will enhance the flavor of a soup (always read the labels carefully), but of all these options, I prefer to add just a pinch of sugar as above. That way the vegetables retain their natural good flavor.

SERVES 6–8

Pictured opposite: Lemony Vegetable Soup with Cream, and Chilled Leek and Potato Soup

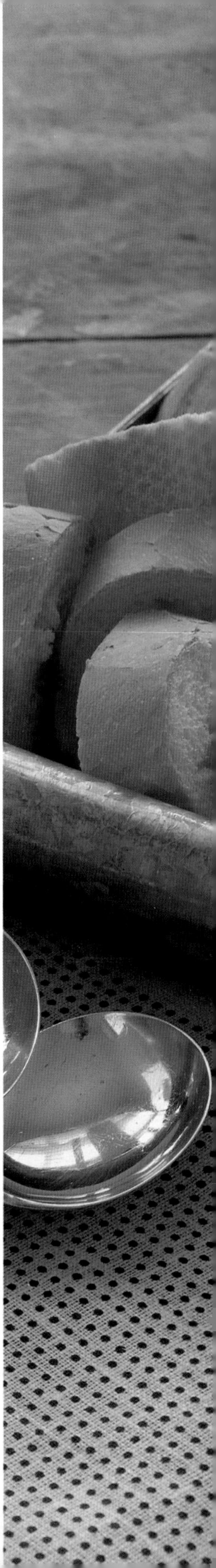

RICH LENTIL SOUP

POTAGE DE PUY

There are many varieties of lentils, all of which can be used to make delicious and nourishing soups. The very best of all are the French lentils de Puy, or Puy lentils, which are small and green. They take longer to cook than many other varieties, but the flavor is definitely worth the wait!

1 cup (8 oz., 250 g) Puy lentils, picked over, washed, and soaked for 3 hours
1 large onion, chopped
2 carrots, diced
1 stalk celery, chopped
1 stalk fennel, chopped
approximately 6 cups (2¹/₂ imp. pints, 1.5 litres) water
2 tablespoons peanut oil
3 garlic cloves, chopped
1 teaspoon curry powder
1 tablespoon tomato paste (purée)
sea salt and freshly ground black pepper
juice of 1 lemon
croutons *or* toasted almonds, to garnish

Drain the lentils and place in a casserole with the onion, carrot, celery, and fennel.

Cover with water, bring to the boil, then simmer for 1½ hours, skimming off any scum when it rises to the surface.

Heat the oil in a small saucepan and sauté the garlic until tender but not browned. Add the curry powder and cook, stirring, for 30 seconds. Stir in the tomato paste and 2 cups of the cooking liquid from the lentils and vegetables. Mix together well, then pour into the pan of lentils.

Pass through a food mill or purée briefly in a blender or food processor — try to achieve a good texture rather than a smooth cream.

Return the soup to the pan to reheat. Season to taste with salt and pepper. Add lemon juice just before serving, and garnish with a scattering of croutons or toasted almonds.

SERVES 6

CABBAGE SOUP, AMIENS-STYLE

LA SOUPE AUX CHOUX D'AMIENS

My sister, Marie-Thérèse, lives with her family in the village of Thézy-Glimont, a few miles from Amiens. She grows her own cabbages, as well as most of her other vegetables. Her house is always full of hungry children, so a soup pot is very handy, and this soup is a favorite. (She also makes a delicious vegetable stew, my version of which can be found on p. 57.)
My grandmother used to say, 'God bless the cabbage, for all good children come from it.' We innocent children used to believe every word!
The high sugar content in cabbage encourages fermentation, so this soup should be eaten on the day it is made.

4 oz. (125 g) butter
1 small green cabbage, about 1 lb. (500 g), washed, drained, and sliced thinly
1 onion, peeled and diced
8 oz. (250 g) potatoes, peeled and cut into thin strips
8 oz. (250 g) carrots, peeled and cut into thin strips
2 celery stalks, cut into thin strips
2 tablespoons yeast extract
1 bouquet garni
10 cups (4 imp. pints, 2.5 litres) water
sea salt and freshly ground black pepper

Heat the butter in a large saucepan. Sauté the vegetables for 8 minutes.
Add the yeast extract, bouquet garni, and water. Boil for 45 minutes. Season to taste with salt and pepper, then remove the bouquet garni.
Serve from a large tureen with crusty whole-wheat (wholemeal) bread for dunking.

VARIATIONS
This soup can be blended in a blender or food processor and served with a little light whipping cream stirred in for a more sophisticated starter.
Replace the carrots with turnips or rutabaga (swedes) for a change.
White cabbage can be used instead of green, if you prefer, but I find the green variety has a more agreeable texture and flavor for this particular dish.

SERVES 8

Pictured left: Rich Lentil Soup

CELERY SOUP WITH GINGER AND ORANGE

BISQUE DE CÉLERI À L'ORANGE

In the past, soups thickened with crushed hard biscuits were known as 'bisques'. Recently, this term has been applied to shellfish soups, but here we have a traditional bisque in which crumbled ginger biscuits add flavor and texture to a piquant chilled soup.

1/3 cup (3 fl. oz., 90 ml) sunflower oil
1 small onion, chopped
1 shallot, chopped
1 head celery (including leaves), coarse stringy parts discarded, stalks separated, washed, and sliced across the grain
1 medium carrot, cut into thin strips
1/2 teaspoon curry powder
3 1/2 cups (28 fl. oz., 875 ml) boiling water
6 whole-wheat (wholemeal) ginger biscuits, crushed with a rolling pin
sea salt and freshly ground black pepper

GARNISH
1 red sweet pepper (capsicum), cut into thin strips and blanched
2 seedless oranges, segmented
fresh coriander leaves, chopped

Heat the oil in a large saucepan and sauté the onion and shallot until soft but not browned. Add the celery and carrots and sauté for a further 4 minutes. Sprinkle in the curry powder and cook, stirring, for 30 seconds.
Pour in the boiling water, stir well, then cover and simmer for 45 minutes.
Place the soup in a blender or food processor and blend until smooth. Return to the saucepan and reheat for 5 minutes.
Stir the biscuit crumbs into the soup. Allow to cool before seasoning with salt and pepper.
Serve chilled, garnished with the red pepper, orange segments, and a sprinkling of coriander.

VARIATION
Vegans might like to add a swirl of soy milk to this soup for a tasty and nourishing lunch or supper.

SERVES 6

CHILLED AVOCADO SOUP WITH TOMATOES AND BASIL

LA SOUPE À L'AVOCAT AUX TOMATES PROVENÇALES

Avocados and tomatoes are both fruit, although we usually serve them as a savory 'vegetable'. This soup from southern France matches the flavor of the tomatoes with the richness of garlic, shallots, olive oil, and basil, and pairs the avocado with creamy-sharp yogurt or fresh goat's cheese.

2 tablespoons (1 fl. oz., 30 ml) olive oil
1 small shallot, chopped
2 garlic cloves, chopped
1 large tomato, skinned, deseeded, and chopped
1 large avocado, pitted, peeled, and chopped
1¼ cups (10 fl. oz., 310 ml) water
sea salt and freshly ground black pepper
⅔ cup (5 fl. oz., 155 ml) plain yogurt *or*
6 oz. (185 ml) fresh goat's cheese
1 tablespoon snipped chives
2 basil leaves, snipped
juice of 1 lemon *or* 2 tablespoons cider vinegar

Heat the oil in a large pan and sauté the shallot and garlic for 1 minute. Stir in the tomato and avocado, and cook gently for 5 minutes.

Add the water, bring to the boil, and simmer for 4 minutes. Season with salt and pepper.

Place in a blender or food processor with the yogurt or goat's cheese and purée until the mixture is smooth and creamy.

Stir in the chives, basil, and lemon juice or vinegar. Swirl well to mix. Pour into a glass bowl and chill well before serving.

SERVES 4

MELON, GINGER, AND CORIANDER SOUP

LA MELONAISE AU GINGEMBRE ET AU CORIANDRE

Use a scented melon, such as the Israeli Ogen melon, for this soup, as a distinct flavor is needed to balance and harmonize with the aromatic ginger and coriander.

1 medium-sized scented melon, halved, deseeded, and skin removed
1 small piece fresh ginger, peeled and grated
1¼ cups (10 fl. oz., 310 ml) white wine
1¼ cups (10 fl. oz., 310 ml) plain yogurt
pinch of sea salt

GARNISH
sprigs of fresh coriander
orange peel, cut in julienne
4 ice cubes

Put the melon flesh, ginger, wine, yogurt, and salt in a blender or food processor. Blend until smooth and creamy. Chill well.

Ladle the chilled soup into individual glass bowls. Decorate with the coriander and orange peel. Float an ice cube in the center of each bowl and serve at once.

Note: Melon flesh, cut into tiny balls or dice, can be added as a garnish if you wish.

SERVES 4

Pictured opposite: Chilled Avocado Soup with Tomatoes and Basil, and Melon, Ginger, and Coriander Soup

CHILLED PEPPER, CUCUMBER, TOMATO, AND ONION SOUP

....

LA BASQUAISE

It was during the reign of Louis XIV that cookery in France began to flourish. The Italian influence of the previous period of the Medicis was replaced by that of Spain, since Louis's queen was a Spanish princess. The court employed Spanish chefs and thus many dishes and styles were introduced to France — such as mayonnaise and all kinds of tomato-based soups and sauces — which have long since been absorbed into classic French cuisine. This recipe has been treasured in my family for centuries. It is rare soup in that it requires no cooking.

8 oz. (250 g) red sweet peppers (capsicums),
coarsely chopped

8 oz. (250 g) green sweet peppers (capsicums),
coarsely chopped

1 lb. (500 g) cucumber, peeled and sliced

1 lb. (500 g) tomatoes, sliced

1 medium onion, chopped

2 garlic cloves, crushed

1¼ cups (10 fl. oz., 310 ml) olive oil

1¼ cups (10 fl. oz., 310 ml) wine vinegar

5 cups (2 imp. pints, 1.25 litres) water

1 tablespoon sea salt

1 tablespoon Demerara (raw) sugar

2 teaspoons paprika

½ teaspoon freshly ground black pepper

8 oz. (250 g) dry French bread

½ cup (2 oz., 60 g) stuffed olives

GARNISH

1 red and 1 green sweet pepper (capsicum), deseeded
and diced in tiny cubes

½ cucumber, skinned and diced into tiny cubes

2 cups (4 oz., 125 g) whole-wheat
(wholemeal) croutons

Put all the soup ingredients in a very large container and leave to marinate overnight in the refrigerator. During this time the flavors will mingle and develop.

Next day, mince or blend the chilled mixture to a coarse purée. Serve in individual bowls with the garnishes on the side, for your guests to help themselves.

Note: This soup freezes well and will also keep for weeks in the refrigerator, so it is worth making in large quantities during summer, when vegetables are cheap and plentiful, and the refreshing quality of this soup can be best appreciated.

SERVES 20

CHILLED PEA SOUP WITH MINT

VELOUTÉ DE POIS VERTS À LA MENTHE

In the region of Clamart, not far from Paris, the most delicious 'petits pois' are grown — as sweet as honey and exquisitely tender. This chilled soup is an ideal way of putting the first peas of summer to use.

2 tablespoons peanut oil

1 small onion, finely chopped

1 shallot, finely chopped

1 small, soft lettuce heart, washed, drained, and torn

2 lbs. (1 kg) fresh green peas, shelled

3½ cups (28 fl. oz., 875 ml) boiling water

⅓ cup (2 oz., 60 g) blanched almonds

⅓ cup (3 fl. oz., 90 ml) hot water

2 mint leaves

sea salt and freshly ground black pepper

toasted, slivered almonds, to garnish

3 additional mint leaves, finely sliced, to garnish

Heat the oil in a large saucepan and sauté the onion and shallot until translucent.

Add the lettuce and peas. Sauté for 5 minutes, then stir in the boiling water, cover, and simmer for 35 minutes.

Place the blanched almonds and hot water in a blender or food processor and blend to a smooth cream. Set aside in a bowl.

Pour the soup into the blender and blend with the 2 mint leaves. Stir this into the almond cream. Cover and chill.

Before serving, season to taste with salt and pepper. Sprinkle with toasted almonds and mint, then serve.

SERVES 6

MORELLO CHERRY SOUP

LA SOUPE AUX CERISE ALSACIENNE

Cherries are native to Asia Minor. It is thought that migratory birds first propagated this lovely fruit in other parts of the world.

3½ cups (28 fl. oz., 875 ml) red wine

¼ cup (3 oz., 90 g) honey

4½ cups (1½ lb., 750 g) fresh Morello cherries, washed, drained, and pitted

good pinch of cinnamon

1 tablespoon potato flour

⅔ cup (5 fl. oz., 155 ml) light cream

3 tablespoons cherry brandy

4 brioches, toasted

Put the wine and honey in a saucepan and bring to the boil. Add the cherries and cinnamon. Stew for 5 minutes, then strain the liquid into a blender or food processor.

Set aside a quarter of the cherries for the garnish. Add the rest to the blender and purée the contents until smooth. Return the mixture to the saucepan and reheat.

In a small bowl, mix the potato flour and cream. Add gradually to the soup, stirring well. Cook for 4 minutes to thicken.

Stir in the remaining whole cherries and brandy.

Chill well before serving in individual bowls with a toasted brioche.

SERVES 4

Pictured above left: Chilled Pepper, Cucumber, Tomato, and Onion Soup

MAIN COURSES

LES PLATS DU JOURS LÉGUMIERS

SPICY CHICKPEAS

POIS CHICHES À LA CATALANE

This traditional dish from the Basque region of France usually contains smoked sausages or bacon. Vegetarians and vegans can make use of delicious smoked tofu to recreate the authentic flavor of the dish — and keep calories lower.

¼ cup (2 fl. oz., 60 ml) olive oil
1 onion, sliced
4 garlic cloves, crushed
1 carrot, sliced
1 stalk fennel, sliced
1 cup (8 oz., 250 g) chickpeas (garbanzos), soaked overnight in cold water, rinsed, and drained
2 cloves
½ cup (4 oz., 125 g) tomato paste (purée)
2–4 green chili peppers, sliced (remove the seeds for a less fiery effect)
1 teaspoon ground cumin
sea salt and freshly ground black pepper
4 oz. (125 g) smoked tofu, cubed

Heat the oil in a large cast-iron pan and sauté the onion, garlic, carrot, and fennel briefly.

Add the chickpeas and cloves, stir, then pour in sufficient water to completely cover. Bring to the boil, cover and simmer for 2½ hours, skimming off any scum as it rises.

Fifteen minutes before cooking ends, stir in the tomato paste and chili peppers. If the mixture is still very liquid at the end of cooking, strain excess liquid off and use as a base for soups — the finished dish should have a quite thick and moist, but not wet, consistency.

Season with cumin, salt, and pepper, and stir in the tofu. Cook gently to warm the tofu until it imparts a smoky flavor to the finished dish.

Serve with plenty of crusty French bread and side dishes of black olives, capers, and pickled gherkins for everyone to help themselves. Non-vegans could also serve it with halved hard-boiled eggs or a sprinkling of grated cheese.

SERVES 6

Pictured on previous pages: Spicy Chickpeas
Pictured right: Classic French Vegetable Stew

VEGETABLE CASSEROLE WITH A CARAWAY BISCUIT TOPPING

CASSEROLE DE LÉGUMES AU CARVI

This is a dish from Alsace, in eastern France. It is good, substantial country fare, best accompanied by beer.

¼ cup (2 fl. oz., 60 ml) oil
2 onions, cut into thin strips
2 garlic cloves, chopped
1 red and 1 green sweet pepper (capsicum), deseeded and cut into thin strips
4 carrots, scrubbed and sliced
2 parsnips, peeled and sliced
⅔ cup (5 fl. oz., 155 ml) dry white wine
⅔ cup (5 fl. oz., 155 ml) water
1 tablespoon yeast extract
sea salt and freshly ground black pepper

BISCUIT (SCONE) TOPPING
2 cups (8 oz., 250 g) whole-wheat (wholemeal) flour
2 teaspoons baking powder
sea salt
1 teaspoon caraway seeds
2 oz. (60 g) polyunsaturated *or* vegan margarine
⅔ cup (5 fl. oz., 155 ml) skim *or* soy milk

Heat the oil in a large saucepan and sauté the onions, garlic, sweet peppers, carrots, and parsnips for 2 minutes. Stir in the wine, water, and yeast extract. Bring to the boil and simmer for 20 minutes so that the vegetables are almost cooked and the sauce thickens.

Taste and season with salt and pepper. Pour the mixture into an earthenware dish and keep warm.

Prepare the biscuit (scone) topping by sifting together the flour, baking powder, and salt in a bowl. Stir in the caraway seeds.

Rub in the margarine, then mix in enough milk to make a smooth, firm dough (reserve at least 2 tablespoons of milk for glazing the biscuits).

Roll out the dough to ½ in. (1 cm) thick and cut 2-in. (5-cm) circles with a cookie or pastry cutter or a glass. Lay the biscuit circles on top of the vegetable mixture, around the edge of the earthenware dish, keeping the center clear. Brush the scones with a little milk.

Bake the casserole in a preheated oven at 400°F (200°C) for 15 minutes, to heat the vegetables well and cook the scone topping. Serve at once.

SERVES 6

CLASSIC FRENCH VEGETABLE STEW

LA RATATOUILLE NIÇOISE

*The French chef of a very famous London hotel once
sacked a young cook because he could not prepare a
ratatouille properly. It caused a kitchen strike at the time.
But all of us older chefs felt the blame lay with the chef for
not being able to teach a dish that is simplicity itself.
Eggplants (aubergines) are wonderfully versatile. Slices
can be floured and seasoned then broiled (grilled) or
fried; eggplant can be baked and then puréed with tahini
to make a pâté; and it can be casseroled, as in a
ratatouille, in which it is the chief ingredient.
Eggplants usually do not need to be skinned — in fact,
the best flavor is in the skin, and its rich purple color is
most pleasing in a dish.
Ratatouille is a favorite dish in France and can be served
in the same earthenware dish in which it is cooked or in
little individual dishes.
In Nice, it is served hot or cold, with black olives as
its only embellishment.*

1/2 cup (4 fl. oz., 125 ml) olive oil

8 oz. (250 g) onions, chopped

3 garlic cloves, chopped

1 lb. (500 g) eggplants (aubergines), cut into
1-in. (2.5-cm) cubes, salted lightly, left for 30 minutes,
then rinsed in cold water, drained, and patted dry

1 lb. (500 g) tomatoes, skinned, deseeded, and chopped

1 lb. (500 g) zucchini (courgettes), thickly sliced

1 red and 1 green sweet pepper (capsicum), deseeded
and cut in 1-in. (2.5-cm) cubes

1 1/4 cups (10 fl. oz., 310 ml) water

1/4 cup (2 oz., 60 g) tomato paste (purée)

sea salt and freshly ground black pepper

2 tablespoons chopped fresh parsley

pinch of chopped fresh basil *or* oregano

12 black olives, to garnish

Heat the oil in a large saucepan and stir-fry the
onion and garlic for 4 minutes.

Add the eggplant, tomatoes, zucchini, and
sweet peppers and stir-fry for 4 minutes. Stir in the
water and tomato paste. Season to taste.

Transfer to an earthenware casserole and bake
at 350°F (180°C) for 40 minutes.

Remove from the oven and sprinkle with the
herbs. Decorate with black olives before serving.

VARIATIONS

A little grated cheese sprinkled onto the dish and
then browned lightly under the broiler (griller)
is very good.

To make more of a meal of the dish, quartered
hard-boiled eggs can be stirred in carefully just
before serving — they go very well with the rich
flavors of the ratatouille.

SERVES 8

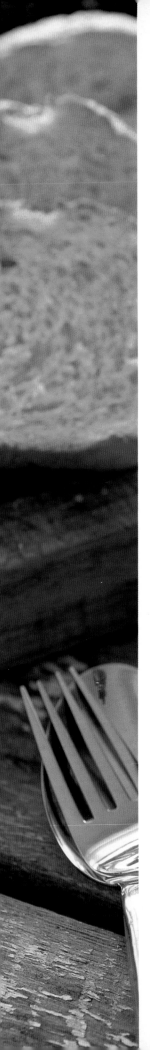

COUNTRY-STYLE POTATO STEW

RAGOÛT DE POMME DE TERRE
THÉZY-GLIMONT

The Battle of the Somme was fought just under half a mile from Thézy-Glimont, where my French family live. The once battle-scarred soil of this rich, marshy plain yields a harvest of the finest vegetables to be sold in the markets of Paris, and the only trenches to be seen these days are dug for the potato crop. I used to dig potato trenches when I was a young man. If I had a dollar for every potato I've pulled out of the ground ...
This recipe, a ragout of potatoes, was a daily ritual at grandmother's house, and she would add whatever other vegetables were plentiful, according to the season. My sister in Thézy-Glimont continues this tradition.

¼ cup (2 fl. oz., 60 ml) olive oil
2 oz. (60 g) butter
1 large onion, chopped
1 garlic clove, crushed
4 stalks celery, cut into equal-sized pieces
2 carrots, cut into equal-sized pieces
1 small turnip, cut into equal-sized pieces
1 rutabaga (swede), cut into equal-sized pieces
1⅓ cups (4 oz., 125 g) shredded cabbage
1 lb. (500 g) new potatoes, quartered
¼ cup (2 oz., 60 g) tomato paste (purée)
5 cups (2 imp. pints, 1.25 litres) water
pinch of chopped fresh thyme
1 bay leaf
4 oz. (125 g) shelled green peas
4 oz. (125 g) runner beans, sliced, *or* snow peas (mangetout)
sea salt and freshly ground black pepper
pinch each of chopped fresh chervil, parsley, marjoram, and mint

In a large casserole, heat the oil and butter and stir-fry the onion and garlic for 4 minutes.

Add the celery, carrots, turnip, swede, and cabbage to the dish, put on the lid to prevent steam escaping, and cook for 5 minutes. Stir well.

Add the potatoes, tomato paste, water, thyme, and bay leaf. Cook, covered, for 20 minutes.

Add the peas and beans or snow peas and cook for a further 10 minutes. Season to taste with salt and pepper.

Serve the stew in large soup bowls, with the rest of the herbs sprinkled on top. Pass around plenty of fresh whole-wheat (wholemeal) bread with which to mop up all the delicious juices.

SERVES 6

SAFFRON-SCENTED VEGETABLE CASSEROLE WITH EGGS

RATA MARSEILLAISE

Here is a dish from the region of Provence in southern France. You might be surprised to discover how such small amounts of saffron and basil are all that are needed to give the flavor, aroma, and character of this region to the dish.

¼ cup (2 fl. oz., 60 ml) olive oil
1 large onion, thinly sliced
4 garlic cloves, chopped
1 stalk celery, chopped
1 stalk fennel, chopped
¼ cup (2 oz., 60 g) tomato paste (purée)
2½ cups (1 imp. pint, 625 ml) water
1 lb. (500 g) new potatoes, scrubbed and quartered
6 strands saffron
1 teaspoon turmeric
1 unsalted vegetable bouillon (stock) cube
2 green chili peppers, deseeded and sliced
4 basil leaves, chopped
3 mint leaves, chopped
4 zucchini (courgettes), thickly sliced
sea salt and freshly ground black pepper
4 eggs, hard-boiled

Heat the oil in a large saucepan and sauté the onion, garlic, celery, and fennel for about 3 minutes without browning. Add the tomato paste and water and boil for 2 minutes before stirring in the potatoes. Simmer for 15 minutes.

Add the saffron, turmeric, bouillon cube, chili peppers, basil, mint, and zucchini. Cook for a further 5 minutes, then taste and season with salt and pepper.

Spoon some of the vegetable mixture into the base of a warmed earthenware serving dish. Cut the eggs in half. Lay them, cut sides down, on top and cover with the remaining vegetable mixture.

Serve with a cooling salad, as this dish can be quite fiery.

VARIATION
Cubes of lightly sautéed smoked tofu could be substituted for the eggs, making this dish ideal for vegans.

SERVES 6

Pictured opposite: Country-style Potato Stew

ONION AND BLUE CHEESE CASSEROLE WITH PRUNES AND WALNUTS

GRATINÉES DES CAUSSES

....

The Causses region of France is wild and rocky, and its people depend on the produce from goats and sheep for much of their nourishment. Of course, the most famous product of all is Roquefort cheese.
This dish uses just a little of that fabulous cheese, yet its flavor is intense and good. A simple dish, it may look at first more like a soup than a casserole, but it is substantial and rich in nutrients. In winter, served with good bread, it's all that's needed to take the chill from your bones.

4 oz. (125 g) butter

1 lb. (500 g) onions, sliced

7 cups (3 imp. pints, 1.75 litres) vegetable stock

4 oz. (125 g) Roquefort cheese

1/3 cup (3 fl. oz., 90 ml) Cognac

2 egg yolks

sea salt and freshly ground black pepper

4 slices French bread

1 cup (4 oz., 125 g) chopped walnuts

8 prunes, pitted and soaked

1 cup (4 oz., 125 g) grated Cantal cheese

Melt half the butter in a large casserole. Add the onions and sauté gently until golden and soft. Pour in the stock and boil for 15 minutes.

Meanwhile, cream together the remaining butter, the Roquefort cheese and Cognac. Beat in 4 tablespoons of the stock to form a smooth paste, then add the egg yolks and beat again.

Remove the casserole from the heat and gradually add the cheese mixture, stirring well. Reheat gently until the stew is thick and creamy. Season with salt and pepper to taste.

Toast the bread and set aside.

Place an equal amount of walnuts and prunes in four individual bowls, then pour over the creamy onion mixture.

Lay a slice of toast in each bowl, sprinkle with some of the cheese, and brown under a hot broiler (griller) until sizzling. Serve at once.

SERVES 4

Pictured above right: Layered Leeks and Potatoes Baked with Cheese and Cream

LAYERED LEEKS AND POTATOES BAKED WITH CHEESE AND CREAM

GRATIN DAUPHINOIS AUX POIREAUX

....

The Dauphiné province of France is noted for its walnuts and dairy produce. This is its most famous regional speciality. It is a simple dish, but one that many people spoil by not paying attention to one important detail: raw potatoes contain an acid that curdles raw milk. If using raw potatoes, the milk must be boiled before it is added to the dish. My method avoids this curdling by scalding the potatoes first, thus neutralizing the acid.

2 lbs. (1 kg) potatoes, washed, peeled, rewashed, and cut into 1/4-in. (6-mm) slices

1 1/4 cups (10 fl. oz., 310 ml) water

2 garlic cloves

2 oz. (60 g) butter

2 eggs, beaten

1 1/4 cups (10 fl. oz., 310 ml) heavy cream

sea salt and freshly ground black pepper

freshly grated nutmeg

6 small leeks, trimmed to remove most of the green part and washed thoroughly

1 1/4 cups (5 oz., 155 g) grated Gruyère cheese

Put the potatoes in a saucepan with the water and scald for 4 minutes. Drain well.

Rub a shallow earthenware baking dish with one cut clove of garlic. Alternatively, crush both garlic cloves and rub over the dish. Cover the dish thickly with the butter.

In a bowl, beat the eggs and cream together. Season with salt, pepper, and nutmeg. If the second garlic clove has not been used, crush it and stir into the mixture.

Boil the leeks for 8 minutes. Drain and gently squeeze out any excess moisture.

Arrange half the potato slices in an overlapping pattern in the bottom of the earthenware dish. Pour half the egg and cream mixture over them, then sprinkle with half the cheese. Arrange the leeks, folded if necessary, over this. Then layer the rest of the potatoes neatly over the leeks. Cover with the rest of the egg and cream mixture and the remaining cheese.

Bake for 1 hour at 375°F (190°C) and serve in the earthenware dish.

VARIATIONS

Almost any other vegetable may be substituted for the leeks, including onions, fennel, and broccoli.

SERVES 6-8

CORNMEAL CROWN FILLED WITH MIXED VEGETABLES

....

COURONNE DE MAÏS À LA FRANÇAISE

Corn has an affinity with sweet peppers (capsicum). In this dish, red and green sweet peppers are used, and I have incorporated both cornmeal and corn kernels.

CORNMEAL CROWN
2¹/₂ cups (1 imp. pint, 625 ml) mixed milk and water

4 oz. (125 g) butter

³/₄ cup (4 oz., 125 g) cornmeal

sea salt and freshly ground black pepper

pinch of ground mace

1 garlic clove, crushed

2 eggs, beaten

MIXED VEGETABLES
¹/₃ cup (3 fl. oz., 90 ml) vegetable oil

1 onion, sliced into strips

1 green and 1 red sweet pepper (capsicum), deseeded and cut into strips

2 cups (4 oz., 125 g) white mushrooms, sliced

¹/₂ cup (3 oz., 90 g) cooked green peas

1 fresh chili pepper, sliced thinly

¹/₂ cup (3 oz., 90 g) cooked corn kernels

¹/₂ cup (3 oz., 90 g) baked beans in tomato sauce

sea salt and freshly ground black pepper

1 teaspoon chopped fresh rosemary, marjoram, *or* parsley, to garnish

In a saucepan, boil the milk and water. Rub 2 table-spoons (1 oz., 30 g) butter into the cornmeal, then add to the boiled milk and water. Stir well. Simmer for 7 to 8 minutes until thick and tender, like porridge. Season to taste with salt, pepper, and mace, and add the garlic. Remove from heat and stir in the egg and half the remaining butter.

With the rest of the butter, liberally grease a salad or ring mold, and pour the mixture in. Smooth the top and leave to set for a few minutes.

When the cornmeal seems firm enough, turn it out onto a flat earthenware dish and place in an oven preheated at 350°F (180°C) for 10 minutes to keep warm while you prepare the vegetables.

Heat the oil in a sauté pan and stir-fry the onion and sweet peppers for 4 minutes. Add the mushrooms and cook for a further 2 minutes.

Stir in the peas, chili pepper, corn, and baked beans, and allow to heat together for 4 minutes. Taste and season with salt and pepper if necessary.

Remove the cornmeal crown from the oven. Fill the center and decorate the edges with the vegetable mixture. Sprinkle with the herbs just before serving.

SERVES 4

ONION TART

LA TOURTE À L'OIGNON

The warmer the climate, the sweeter the onion. This is why Spanish onions are still imported into France, despite the protests of our farmers. From a chef's point of view, imported onions certainly are the best, but Brittany onions are very good, too. Bretons often eat them as we would an apple — raw, with just a hunk of bread to accompany them. The health-giving antiseptic properties of the onion are well known, so perhaps this will 'keep the doctor away' — but the effect on the breath might keep everyone else away, too!

Onions are used to enhance almost every savory dish, it seems. They are also served as a vegetable in their own right, and as a main course too, when stuffed with a suitable filling or used to fill a quiche, as in this recipe.

1 quantity shortcrust pastry (see p. 158)

½ cup (4 oz., 125 g) mixed butter and oil

8 oz. (250 g) onions, sliced

1 cup (4 oz., 125 g) grated Gruyère cheese

3 eggs, beaten

½ cup (4 fl. oz., 125 ml) heavy cream

sea salt and freshly ground black pepper

freshly grated nutmeg

6 black olives, pitted

Roll out the pastry to ¼ in. (6 mm) thickness and use it to line a well-greased 8-in. (20-cm) quiche pan. The pastry should come slightly above the rim of the pan — crimp this edge into a fluted pattern with your thumb and forefinger.

Heat the butter and oil in a saucepan and gently sauté the onions for 8 minutes without browning. Remove from the heat.

In a bowl, mix together the cheese, eggs, cream, salt, pepper, and nutmeg.

Stir this into the onions. Pour the mixture into the pastry case and bake for 30 minutes in a preheated oven at 400°F (200°C).

Decorate the tart with the olives and serve hot or cold.

SERVES 6-8

Pictured opposite: Onion Tart

ONIONS IN RED WINE WITH ROASTED CHICKPEAS

OIGNONS BORDELAIS

The contrast of little onions simmered in a rich claret sauce and the crunch of roasted chickpeas (garbanzos) makes this simple dish a gastronomic treat.

¼ cup (2 fl. oz., 60 ml) walnut oil

1 lb. (500 g) baby onions, peeled and left whole

2 garlic cloves, crushed

2 tablespoons tomato paste (purée)

2 tablespoons honey

1 teaspoon mixed spice

1 cup (8 fl. oz., 250 ml) red wine, preferably Bordeaux

2 large tomatoes, skinned, deseeded, and diced

1 sprig thyme

5 basil leaves

½ cup (3 oz., 90 g) raisins

½ cup (4 fl. oz., 125 ml) water

sea salt and freshly ground black pepper

1 cup (8 oz., 250 g) chickpeas (garbanzos), soaked for 8 hours or overnight, rinsed, and drained

Heat the oil in a large saucepan and sauté the onions until golden.

Add the garlic, tomato paste, honey, mixed spice, and wine, and boil until the wine has almost evaporated and the mixture is syrupy.

Stir in the tomatoes, thyme, basil, and raisins, then add the water so that it is just level with the other ingredients. Add salt and pepper to taste and simmer for 20 minutes.

Meanwhile, preheat the oven to its hottest temperature. Place the drained chickpeas on a baking sheet (tray) and roast for about 12 minutes, moving them about frequently to ensure even cooking. They should be golden-brown, with a nutty aroma, but with no hint of scorching.

Spoon the cooked onions into the center of a warmed serving dish and arrange the roasted chickpeas around the edge. Serve with brown rice or thick chunks of fresh whole-wheat (wholemeal) bread to mop up the juices.

SERVES 6

BASQUE CHICKPEA STEW

POT AU FEU DE POIS CHICHE BASQUAISE

Don't be daunted by the long list of ingredients for this recipe. Its preparation is simplicity itself, and the wonderful aroma of the blend of spices and vegetables that will fill your kitchen is well worth it. The cuisine of the Basque region has a Spanish–Moorish influence, hence the exotic flavors evoked in this dish.

1 medium onion, chopped
¼ cup (2 fl. oz., 60 ml) olive oil
1 garlic clove, crushed
1 teaspoon ground cumin
1 teaspoon curry powder *or* garam masala
¼ teaspoon ground cardamom
¼ teaspoon ground cumin
pinch of ground allspice
1 small red chili pepper, deseeded and finely chopped
1 tablespoon finely chopped fresh ginger
1 tablespoon whole-wheat (wholemeal) flour
1½ cups (12 fl. oz., 375 ml) vegetable stock
2 medium carrots, chopped
2 medium potatoes, chopped
½ small cauliflower, separated into florets
8 oz. (225 g) green beans, cut into short lengths

1 medium apple, chopped
1 can (15 oz., 475 g) chickpeas (garbanzos), drained
7 fl. oz. (225 ml) plain yogurt
sea salt and freshly ground black pepper
¼ cup (1 oz., 30 g) pine nuts
1 tablespoon chopped fresh coriander

Heat the oil in a large, deep saucepan and sauté the onion until soft and translucent. If it browns very slightly, this does not matter. Add the garlic, the ground spices, the chili pepper and ginger, and sauté gently for a minute or so to bring out the flavors. Add the flour and cook, stirring, for a minute to make a smooth roux. Gradually add the vegetable stock and heat until the mixture simmers and becomes a thin sauce.

Add the carrots, potatoes, cauliflower, and beans and simmer together until everything is tender and the sauce has thickened more.

Add the apple and chickpeas. Stir in most of the yogurt, reserving a little for serving, and heat through but do not allow to boil as it may curdle. Season to taste.

Toast the pine nuts briefly in a dry saucepan.

Serve the *pot au feu* on a large dish, drizzled with the remaining yogurt, and sprinkled with the toasted pine nuts and fresh coriander.

SERVES 4

RICH EGGPLANT PUDDING

LE CLAFOUTU AUX AUBERGINES

*All lovers of French cuisine will have heard of clafoutis,
but few will know how to make a clafoutu. Well, here is
my Aunt Galibert's version as an introduction.*

I quince, cored, peeled, and sliced
2 large eggplants (aubergines), sliced, washed, and
patted dry
¼ cup (2 oz., 60 g) toasted crushed almonds
¼ cup (2 fl. oz., 60 ml) walnut oil
4 garlic cloves, crushed
I large onion, sliced into rings
¼ cup (2 oz., 60 g) softened butter

BATTER
½ cup (2 oz., 60 g) whole-wheat (wholemeal) flour
3 eggs, beaten
1½ cups (12 fl. oz., 375 ml) milk
sea salt and freshly ground black pepper
I teaspoon Demerara (raw) sugar
freshly grated nutmeg

I large beefsteak tomato, thinly sliced
I tablespoon dark rum

Boil the quince slices for 10 minutes, then drain
them well.

Coat the eggplant slices in crushed almonds.

Heat the oil in a saucepan and sauté the
eggplant slices on both sides until just softened.
Drain well and reserve. In the same oil, sauté the
garlic and onion until softened. Drain and reserve.

Grease a rectangular ovenproof dish with the
butter and set aside.

To prepare the batter, beat the flour, eggs, and
milk together in a bowl. Season with salt, pepper,
sugar, and nutmeg. Pour the batter into the
greased dish.

On top of the batter, arrange rows of quince,
eggplant, onion rings, and tomato.

Place in a preheated oven and cook at 350°F
(180°C) for 45 minutes. Remove from the oven
and sprinkle with the rum.

Serve hot or cold, cut crossways into slices so
that everyone gets some of each of the vegetables.

SERVES 4

Pictured left: Basque Chickpea Stew

SAVORY ROLLS
WITH ASPARAGUS
AND GOAT'S CHEESE

LES CANNELONS DE NAPOLÉON

*This was cooked for Napoleon by his chef Laguipière and
combines the Italian influence, so strong in Napoleon's
homeland of Corsica, with French gastronomy. The poor
chef was just one of many who died — of frostbite —
during Napoleon's disastrous Russian campaign.*

NOODLES
2 cups (8 oz., 250 g) whole-wheat (wholemeal) semolina
2 eggs, beaten
2 tablespoons vegetable oil
2 tablespoons water
pinch of sea salt

FILLING
8 oz. (250 g) fresh goat's cheese
I egg yolk
sea salt and freshly ground black pepper
1½ cups (8 oz., 250 g) cooked asparagus

COATING
½ cup (2 oz., 60 g) whole-wheat (wholemeal) flour
2 eggs, beaten
¾ cup (3 oz., 90 g) finely crushed almonds
oil, for deep-frying

Combine all the noodle ingredients to form a
pliable dough. Allow to rest for 20 minutes.

Meanwhile, cream together the goat's cheese
and egg yolk. Season to taste with salt and pepper.

Roll out the dough on a board dusted with
semolina. Cut into 8 rectangles, each measuring
4 x 2 in. (10 x 5 cm).

Place a little of the cheese, rolled in a small
sausage shape, on each rectangle of dough. Leave
some room around the edges. Into the cheese,
press two pieces of asparagus that have been cut to
the same length as the cheese.

Wet the edges of the dough and roll into a
tube, then pinch and fold the ends to seal in the
filling completely.

Roll these *cannelons* in the flour, then the beaten
eggs, then the crushed nuts.

Heat oil in a saucepan and deep-fry the *cannelons*
until golden all over — about 5 minutes.

Serve hot or cold with dips of your choice and
two salads, one green, one tomato, both with
garlic dressing.

SERVES 4

A Medley of Macaroni and Vegetable Strips with Snow Peas

Macaroni Champs Elysées

Pasta is delicious served in summer as a salad with fresh, lightly cooked vegetables or with pulses. (It is just as good in winter, too, of course!) When you need a carbohydrate-based side dish that is not too heavy, a pasta salad, hot or cold, is ideal. Macaroni is a useful size and shape to mingle with the pleasantly 'al dente' vegetables. Always cook the pasta in plenty of salted water and drain very well. Plenty of lemon juice is needed in this dish to really sharpen up the flavor of the mild pasta and fresh vegetables.

Extra pasta will keep well in the refrigerator for up to a week. Before use, reheat it in boiling water for a few minutes, then drain well and sauté in butter before adding your chosen sauce.

2 carrots, peeled and cut into fine strips
4 stalks celery, cut into fine strips
4 oz. (125 g) green beans, ends removed
1 small red sweet pepper (capsicum), deseeded and cut into fine strips
4 oz. (125 g) snow peas (mangetout), ends removed
1 cup (5 oz., 155 g) macaroni
4 oz. (125 g) butter
sea salt and freshly ground black pepper
1 onion, sliced into thin rings
1/3 cup (3 fl. oz., 90 ml) light whipping cream
juice of 1 lemon
1 cup (4 oz., 125 g) grated Gruyère cheese

Put the carrots, celery, beans, sweet pepper, and snow peas in boiling salted water and blanch for 5 minutes. Drain well.

Cook the macaroni in boiling salted water for 12 minutes or until *al dente*. Rinse in cold water, then drain well.

Heat the butter in a large saucepan and toss the blanched vegetables in it. Season with salt and pepper. Lightly toss the vegetables with the macaroni, then place in a serving dish.

In the butter remaining in the saucepan, sauté the onion for 4 minutes and drain off any excess butter. Stir the cream into the onions and bring to the boil. Add the lemon juice.

Stir this mixture into the vegetables and pasta. Stir the cheese in at the last minute and serve.

SERVES 4

Spiral Pasta with Cashew Nut Balls

Pâtes Spirales aux Noix d'Acajou

I have used spiral pasta for this dish but any shaped pasta is good. The sauce and the cashew nut balls can be made up to two days in advance, if kept covered in the refrigerator. Instead of cashew nuts, you can use cooked chickpeas, peanuts, pine nuts, or a mixture of them all.

CASHEW NUT BALLS
2 1/2 cups (10 oz., 310 g) fresh cashew nuts
1 cup (2 oz., 60 g) whole-wheat (wholemeal) breadcrumbs, stale but not dried
2 eggs, lightly beaten
1 garlic clove, crushed
sea salt and freshly ground black pepper
olive oil, for frying

SAUCE
1 oz. (30 g) butter
1 large onion, chopped
1 garlic clove, crushed
4 large tomatoes, skinned and roughly chopped
2 tablespoons tomato paste (purée)
2 teaspoons chopped fresh oregano *or* basil
1 1/2 cups (12 fl. oz., 375 ml) water

sea salt and freshly ground black pepper
8 oz. (250 g) whole-wheat (wholemeal) spiral pasta

In a blender or food processor, blend the cashew nuts until quite fine but not powdered. In a bowl, mix them with the breadcrumbs, egg, garlic, and seasoning, and mold into walnut-sized balls. Add extra breadcrumbs if necessary.

Heat the oil in a skillet or frying pan and sauté the nut balls until golden-brown. Set aside.

For the sauce, heat the butter in a saucepan and sauté the onion and garlic until soft but not browned. Add the tomatoes, tomato paste, oregano or basil, and water, and bring to the boil. Reduce the heat and allow to simmer gently until thickened. Season to taste.

Put the pasta in boiling water. Just before it is cooked, stir the nut balls into the sauce and allow to heat through.

Drain the pasta and put on a large serving plate. Pour the sauce and nut balls over and serve.

SERVES 4

Pictured opposite: Medley of Macaroni and Vegetable Strips with Snow Peas

COUSCOUS WITH SPINACH
AND WALNUTS

COMPOTE D'ÉPINARD AU COUSCOUS

The cuisine of the south of France, especially around the port of Marseilles, has a cosmopolitan flavor, reflecting the association between France and its former colonies in Africa. Couscous is one of my favorite dishes of this type. It is very popular amongst young Parisians at the moment.

¼ cup (2 fl. oz., 60 ml) walnut oil

2 lbs. (1 kg) fresh spinach, washed, coarse stems and
damaged leaves discarded

1 cup (4 oz., 125 g) walnuts

⅔ cup (4 oz., 125 g) diced dried dates

2 garlic cloves, chopped

juice of 1 lemon

sea salt and freshly ground black pepper

freshly ground mace

1 cup (4 oz., 125 g) couscous

1 tablespoon olive oil

1¼ cups (10 fl. oz., 310 ml) water *or* vegetable stock

1 red *or* green chili pepper, deseeded and sliced

extra sea salt

pinch of ground cumin

Heat the walnut oil in a large saucepan and add the spinach. Cook, stirring, until the leaves wilt. Add the walnuts and dates.

Blend the garlic and lemon juice together. Stir this into the spinach. Cover and simmer for 15 minutes before seasoning with salt, pepper, and mace.

Rub the couscous with the olive oil, then place in a saucepan and sauté for 1 minute. Pour in the water or stock, add the chili pepper, and cook for 5 minutes before transferring to an earthenware dish. Dry in a preheated oven at 400°F (200°C) for 10 to 12 minutes, fluffing with a fork occasionally to separate the grains. Season with salt and cumin.

Make a ring with the couscous on a warmed serving plate and pile the spinach mixture into the center. Serve at once.

SERVES 6

Rice and Mushroom Pastry Roll

Coulibiac de Riz aux Champignons Baronne de Juniac

During my travels in Russia before and during World War II, I encountered many versions of the traditional coulibiac. This dish had been introduced into French cuisine many years before by French chefs who worked for the nobility in Russia before the 1917 Revolution, but it was primarily the salmon version that was adopted into haute cuisine.

A variation on a well-known theme is always permitted to a composer who knows his art, and, therefore, I proudly present my vegetarian version of this classic dish. I am so delighted with its outcome that I have dedicated it to my esteemed patrons, the Baron and Baroness de Juniac, whose palates I trust most amongst all my clientele.

6 cabbage leaves

2 oz. (60 g) butter

1/4 cup (2 fl. oz., 60 ml) olive oil

1 onion, chopped

2 garlic cloves, chopped

2/3 cup (5 oz., 155 g) long-grain brown rice

2 1/2 cups (1 imp. pint, 625 ml) water

3 eggs, beaten

sea salt and freshly ground black pepper

1 tablespoon each chopped fresh tarragon and parsley

1/2 cup (2 oz., 60 g) toasted slivered almonds

1 1/2 lbs. (750 g) puff pastry (see p. 159) *or* brioche dough (see p. 149)

2 cups (4 oz., 125 g) white mushrooms, sliced

4 tomatoes, skinned, deseeded, and quartered

4 eggs, hard-boiled and quartered

4 oz. (125 g) Gruyère cheese, sliced

Scald the cabbage leaves in boiling water for 3 minutes, then refresh in cold water before draining thoroughly.

In a large saucepan, heat the butter and oil and stir-fry the onion and garlic for 2 minutes. Add the rice and stir to allow it to absorb the fat. Pour in the water, cover tightly with a lid, and boil gently for 40 to 45 minutes or until the water has been absorbed and the rice is tender.

When the rice is cooked, remove it from the heat, blend in two-thirds of the beaten egg, and season with salt and pepper. Allow to cool before stirring in the tarragon, parsley, and almonds.

Lightly flour a large pastry board and roll out the dough into a rectangle that measures approximately 12 x 18 in. (30 x 45 cm).

Lay 3 cabbage leaves out on the dough. Cover the center, taking an area of 6 x 12 in. (15 x 30 cm), with a layer of half the rice mixture, then sprinkle with half the mushrooms and tomatoes. Cover with the remaining rice, then the mushrooms and tomatoes. Top with the hard-boiled egg quarters and the cheese, and cover with the 3 remaining cabbage leaves.

Blend the remaining egg with 4 tablespoons of water. Bring the two long sides of the pastry up over the filling and use a little of the egg wash to seal the edges together. Bring the ends up and seal them to close up the pastry roll.

Very carefully, turn the roll over and place it on a greased baking sheet (tray) so that the seams are underneath. Brush the top with the rest of the egg wash and use a fork to make a decorative criss-cross pattern.

Bake in a preheated oven at 400°F (200°C) for 30 minutes — the pastry should puff up and turn a delicious golden-brown. Serve hot with a tomato salad or a curly endive salad and lemon dressing.

Variation

Instead of cabbage leaves, thin pancakes can be used for a more substantial dish.

Note: If you are unsure about filling and rolling the coulibiac, try the following technique the first time you prepare the dish.

When the dough is rolled out, use a knife to lightly mark a rectangle in the middle about 3 in. (8 cm) from the edges. Cut out squares from each corner of the rectangle to the edge of the dough. Place the filling in the rectangle and fold up the sides and ends as instructed above. If you like, you can re-roll the dough left over from the trimmed squares and cut it into thin strips. Use egg wash to attach the strips to the coulibiac in a criss-cross or other decorative pattern.

SERVES 4

Pictured above left: Couscous with Spinach and Walnuts

Oriental-Style Vegetables with Noodles

Les Nouilles à la Julienne de Légumes Saint Jérome

Shop-bought whole-wheat (wholemeal) noodles can be used in this stir-fry dish if time is short.

NOODLES
2 cups (8 oz., 250 g) whole-wheat
(wholemeal) semolina
2 eggs, beaten
2 tablespoons vegetable oil
2 tablespoons water
pinch of sea salt

VEGETABLES
2 carrots, peeled and cut into matchsticks
1 small turnip, peeled and cut into matchsticks
1 potato, peeled and cut into matchsticks
4 stalks celery, cut into matchsticks
1/2 red and 1/2 green sweet pepper (capsicum),
cut into matchsticks
4 oz. (125 g) green or string beans, sliced
1/3 cup (3 fl. oz., 90 ml) pineapple juice
1 small piece fresh ginger, peeled and sliced
2 tablespoons soy sauce
1/4 cup (2 oz., 60 g) mixed oil and butter
2 cups (4 oz., 125 g) bean sprouts
2 cups (4 oz., 125 g) white mushrooms
sea salt and freshly ground black pepper

Combine the noodle ingredients into a pliable dough. Rest for 20 minutes. On a board dusted with semolina, roll into a 10 x 5 in. (25 x 12 cm), 1/8–1/4 in. (3–6 mm) thick rectangle. Dust the surface with semolina and carefully roll up lengthways. Cut the roll at 1/4-in. (6-mm) intervals. Place these long noodles onto a baking sheet (tray) lined with waxproof (greaseproof) paper dusted with semolina. Leave to dry out for a time then cook in boiling, salted water for 4 minutes only. Refresh in cold water, drain well. Chop into short lengths.

Blanch the vegetables in boiling water for 4 minutes. Refresh in cold water, then drain.

Blend the pineapple juice with the ginger, soy sauce, salt and pepper. Set aside. Heat the oil and butter in a large pan. Stir-fry the noodles and vegetables, remove from the heat and stir in the mushrooms and bean sprouts. Pour the sauce over and garnish with fresh coriander (cilantro).

SERVES 6

Lentil Loaf with Yogurt and Herbs

Pain de Lentilles à l'Aigre-Doux

This rich, rustic loaf is a traditional recipe that may have been introduced to France by the Romans — they believed this nourishing food induced indolence, so perhaps they hoped to quell the rebellious natives with it!

2 oz. (60 g) butter
1 cup (8 oz., 250 g) red lentils, picked over
1/4 cup (2 fl. oz., 60 ml) sunflower oil
1 medium onion, chopped
2 garlic cloves, crushed
2 teaspoons curry powder
1/4 cup (2 oz., 60 g) tomato paste (purée)
2/3 cup (5 fl. oz., 155 ml) dry white wine
sea salt and freshly ground black pepper
1 tablespoon chopped fresh basil
1 tablespoon chopped fresh coriander
1 small green chili pepper, chopped
2 large eggs, beaten
1/3 cup (3 fl. oz., 90 ml) sour cream

Grease a large loaf pan with the butter, then place the pan in the refrigerator to harden the butter coating.

Place the lentils in a saucepan with double their volume of water. Bring to the boil and cook for 15 minutes until softened and quite dry. Remove from the heat and place in a mixing bowl.

Heat the oil in a saucepan and sauté the onion and garlic for 2 minutes to soften. Stir in the curry powder and cook briefly, then add the tomato paste and wine. Boil for 5 minutes.

Beat this mixture into the lentils, then season to taste with salt and pepper, and add the basil, coriander, and chili pepper.

In a small bowl, beat together the eggs and cream, then stir into the lentils.

Fill the loaf pan with this mixture. Place in a water bath or bain marie and bake in a preheated oven at 375°F (190°C) for 45 minutes. Let stand for 12 minutes, unmold and serve hot or cold with a rice salad for a protein-balanced main meal.

SERVES 6

Pictured opposite: Oriental-style Vegetables with Noodles

CAULIFLOWER SOUFFLÉ

SOUFFLÉ DE CHOU-FLEUR PICARDIE

Cauliflower cheese is a favorite standby dish, yet if you have the ingredients for it, then you will almost certainly have the ingredients for this just as easy but much more special dish. To give extra protein, I have used soy milk for the sauce, but ordinary milk could be used instead.

1 small cauliflower, separated into florets and washed well

3 oz. (90 g) butter

1 teaspoon mustard seeds

1/2 cup (2 oz., 60 g) whole-wheat (wholemeal) flour

1 1/4 cups (10 fl. oz., 310 ml) soy milk

sea salt and freshly ground black pepper

freshly grated nutmeg

4 eggs plus 1 egg white

2 cups (8 oz., 250 g) grated Gruyère cheese

1/2 cup (2 oz., 60 g) ground, toasted peanuts

pinch of sea salt

Bring a saucepan of salted water to the boil and cook the cauliflower for 12 minutes, then drain and mash coarsely.

Heat two-thirds of the butter in a saucepan and sauté the mustard seeds briefly. Stir in the flour to make a dry roux. Cook gently before gradually adding the milk, stirring all the time, to make a thick, smooth sauce. Season with salt, pepper, and nutmeg. Remove from the heat.

Beat one whole egg into the sauce. Separate the remaining three eggs and beat the yolks into the sauce. Reserve all the egg whites in a clean bowl.

Grease a 1-quart (1¾-imp. pint, 1-litre) soufflé dish with the remaining butter, then sprinkle with a little of the cheese.

Stir the rest of the cheese into the sauce, along with the mashed cauliflower and peanuts.

Whisk the egg whites and a pinch of salt until very stiff. Fold gradually into the sauce mixture, taking care not to beat out all the bubbles. It is better to undermix than overmix.

Fill the soufflé dish with the mixture. Mark the top with a criss-cross pattern, then run the back of a spoon around the rim of the dish. This helps the soufflé rise evenly. Place the dish on a baking sheet (tray) and cook in a preheated oven at 400°F (200°C) for 20 to 30 minutes. The soufflé should have risen and be golden but still slightly wobbly when moved. This gives a creamy center.

Serve straight from the oven — your guests should always wait for the soufflé, not it for them.

SERVES 6

COUNTRY VEGETABLE OMELET

OMELETTE VENDÉENNE

The province of Vendée was the last bastion of the monarchy during the French Revolution, which says much about the character of the people of the region. The gastronomy of the area is very distinctive too, and thrives in such towns as La Rochelle, Sables d'Olonnes, and Fontenay-le-Comte, where I was born during World War I. The rosé wine of the area is the finest in France and makes a perfect accompaniment to this dish. There are over a hundred different types of omelet in France, all stemming from simple country cooking. This one is a flat, pancake-like omelet.

4 oz. (125 g) butter

1/2 cup (4 fl. oz., 125 ml) olive oil

1 small onion, chopped

2 cups (2 oz., 60 g) washed and shredded spinach

1 small potato, cooked and diced

1 cup (2 oz., 60 g) cooked and diced artichokes

1/3 cup (2 oz., 60 g) cooked and sliced green beans

sea salt and freshly ground black pepper

12 eggs, beaten and seasoned with sea salt and freshly ground black pepper

grated cheese (optional)

fresh parsley leaves, to garnish

In a skillet or frying pan, heat half the butter and half the oil. Stir-fry the onion and spinach for 4 minutes.

Add the potatoes, artichokes, and beans and cook together for a further 4 minutes. Remove from the heat and season with salt and pepper. Set aside in a bowl.

In an omelet pan, heat 1 tablespoon of the butter and 1 tablespoon of the oil. Reheat a quarter of the vegetable mixture in this. When it is sizzling, immediately add a quarter of the beaten eggs. Stir, allowing the omelet to cook on one side, then either turn over to cook on the other side or brown under a broiler (griller). Sprinkle grated cheese on before browning, if you wish.

Repeat to make three more omelets. Sprinkle with parsley and serve.

SERVES 4

Pictured above right: Pumpkin Risotto

PUMPKIN RISOTTO

POTIRON À LA PROVENÇALE

Here is a pumpkin supper dish — this time a fragrant rice dish redolent with the garlic aromas of southern France, whence it comes.

4 oz. (125 g) butter

1 large red onion, chopped

4 garlic cloves, crushed

scant ¹/₂ cup (4 oz., 125 g) brown rice

2¹/₂ cups (1 imp. pint, 625 ml) vegetable stock

3 lbs. (1.5 kg) pumpkin, peeled, deseeded, and chopped into ¹/₂-in. (1-cm) chunks

1 bouquet garni

¹/₃ cup (2 oz., 60 g) seedless raisins

¹/₄ cup (1 oz., 30 g) slivered almonds, to garnish

1 tablespoon parsley leaves, to garnish

Heat the butter in a metal casserole and gently sauté the onion and garlic until tender. Add the rice and stir until the butter has impregnated the grains.

Add the stock, then stir in the pumpkin and bouquet garni. Cover and cook in a preheated oven at 400°F (200°C) for 35 minutes or until the rice is cooked and the liquid absorbed. About 5 minutes before the end of the cooking time, stir in the seedless raisins.

Remove the casserole from the oven, discard the bouquet garni, and check the seasoning. Sprinkle with the almonds and parsley and serve with a simple tomato salad.

SERVES 4

PROVENÇAL VEGETABLE BAKE

GRATIN D'AIX EN PROVENCE

Time and time again throughout this book, you will find I use the term 'stir-fry' for cooking fresh vegetables. This is a technique that has entered modern French cookery from Oriental cuisine, where vegetables are cooked quickly in a little oil, just to the point where they are no longer raw but still retain their crispy texture, all their flavor, and all their vitamins. It is a quick and easy technique to perfect — the important thing is to keep stirring so the vegetables are cooked evenly, and to slice vegetables evenly and finely and put them in the pan in the order of the length of time they take to cook. (For example, you would put carrots in before mushrooms.)

This dish is inspired by the colors and flavors of Provence. I like to think that it would have been enjoyed by the artist Paul Cézanne, who was born in Aix, and whose sister, Rose, married my ancestor Maxime Conil.

8 oz. (225 g) new potatoes, thinly sliced

1 fennel bulb, thinly sliced

olive oil

1 medium onion, thinly sliced

2 large eggplants (aubergines), thinly sliced, soaked in cold water for 30 minutes, drained, and patted dry

4 zucchini (courgettes), thinly sliced

2 large tomatoes, thinly sliced

8 oz. (225 g) firm goat's cheese, crumbled

12 black olives, pitted and chopped

2 sun-dried tomatoes, chopped

2 oz. (60 g) dried whole-wheat (wholemeal) breadcrumbs

1 tablespoon each chopped fresh basil and thyme

sea salt and freshly ground black pepper

Boil the potatoes and fennel separately until just tender. Refresh in cold water, drain, pat dry.

Heat the oven to 400°F (200°C).

Heat a little olive oil in a heavy-based saucepan and stir-fry the onion for 2 minutes, then add the fennel, eggplants, and zucchini, and fry for a further 3 minutes. Season to taste.

In a large, greased earthenware dish, place a layer each of half the potatoes, half the vegetable mixture, then half the tomatoes. Sprinkle with half the goat's cheese, olives, sun-dried tomatoes, basil, and thyme. Repeat with the remaining ingredients. Top with the breadcrumbs and drizzle a little olive oil over the top.

Bake in the preheated oven at 400°F (200°C) for about 25 minutes or until the top is golden and sizzling. Serve immediately.

SERVES 6

FRENCH RIVIERA–STYLE PIZZA

LA PISSALADIÈRE CÔTE D'AZUR

Generations of Italians have lived on the Riviera ever since Nice and the province of Savoy belonged to Italy, and they have had a huge influence on the gastronomy of the region. But the French cook is a tough nut to crack and will always have a say in a dish, making an amendment here, adding an ingredient there, until the dish becomes part of French cuisine. A notable example is pissaladière. In name and content its origin as a pizza is recognizable, but the adaptations that have been made over the years have rendered it truly French.

Normal bread dough makes a perfect base for pissaladière, just as it does for pizza. Crusty French bread makes a good base too, and even the traditional English milk bun. I am now considering what might be the best base of all (a croissant dough mix, perhaps?) but to tell you more would be giving too much away. So here, for now, is the precious pissaladière recipe I used to prepare at the Hotel des Pins in Cannes in 1937.

1 lb. (500 g) bread dough (see p. 144) *or* brioche dough (see p. 149)

⅓ cup (3 fl. oz., 90 ml) olive oil

2 cups (8 oz., 250 g) button mushrooms, cleaned and patted dry

juice of 1 lemon

8 stuffed olives, sliced

4 large tomatoes, skinned, deseeded, and sliced

1 large onion, sliced

4 oz. (125 g) mozzarella cheese, sliced

sea salt and freshly ground black pepper

chopped fresh oregano

extra olive oil

Roll the dough into a ball and brush it with olive oil. With your hands, flatten and enlarge the ball until you have a disc about 10 in. (25 cm) in diameter. Place the dough on an oiled baking sheet and leave to prove for 15 minutes. If your oven is too small to accommodate one big pizza, make two, or even four, small pissaladières.

Marinate the mushrooms in lemon juice for 5 minutes, then slice.

Place the toppings on the dough in this order: first, the mushrooms, the olives, then the tomatoes, onion, and, finally, the cheese.

Bake in a preheated oven at 400°F (200°C) for 15 to 20 minutes. Sprinkle with salt, pepper, oregano, and a little extra oil before serving.

SERVES 4

Pictured opposite: Provençal Vegetable Bake

SIDE DISHES

LES PLATS DE GARNITURE

Snow Peas with Sesame Seeds

Les Mangetouts aux Graines de Sésame

In all the fashionable restaurants, there is a craze for snow peas (mangetout). To comply with this trend, I offer you a simple way of preparing them, which will impress your fashion-conscious guests. All kinds of flavorings are suited to these little pea pods. They are delicious served hot or cold. My version, with strips of ginger, fennel, carrots, and celery, served hot, complements the fresh color and flavor of this lightly cooked vegetable.

2 lbs. (1 kg) snow peas (mangetout), topped and tailed

1 carrot, cut into julienne

2 stalks celery, cut into julienne

2 oz. (60 g) fennel, cut into julienne

2 oz. (60 g) butter

1 small onion, sliced

1 oz. (30 g) fresh ginger, peeled and chopped

sea salt and freshly ground black pepper

1 teaspoon Demerara (raw) sugar

1 tablespoon soy sauce

1 teaspoon wine vinegar

2 teaspoons sesame seeds, lightly toasted

Put the snow peas into boiling salted water and cook for 5 minutes. Drain.

Blanch the carrots, celery, and fennel for 3 minutes in boiling water. Drain well.

In a sauté pan, heat the butter and stir-fry the onion, ginger, and julienne vegetables for about 4 minutes. Add the snow peas to reheat.

When the vegetables are all heated through, season to taste with salt and pepper and stir in the sugar, soy sauce, and vinegar. Cook for 2 minutes more, stirring all the time, sprinkle with sesame seeds, then serve immediately on a heated plate.

Note: The ginger could first be blended with the soy sauce and 2 tablespoons oil in a blender or food processor if it seems at all dry and tough. This 'spreads' the flavor more evenly throughout the dish, too.

If you cut the carrots, celery, and fennel into *very fine* julienne, you can omit the blanching procedure.

SERVES 4

Pictured on previous pages: Snow Peas with Sesame Seeds, and Potato Cake

Potato Cake

Gâteau de Pommes de Terre

This wonderfully simple dish makes a pleasant change from the more usual gratin-type dishes made of sliced potato. Do not rinse the potatoes when sliced, as you would for a gratin, as the starch is needed to hold them together in a neat gâteau shape.

2 oz. (60 g) butter *or* vegetable margarine

2 lbs. (1 kg) potatoes, scrubbed or peeled and thinly sliced

sea salt and freshly ground black pepper

freshly grated nutmeg

1 large garlic clove, crushed

Melt the butter or margarine and brush over a round 8-in. (20-cm) ovenproof gratin dish.

Place a neat layer of potatoes in the base. Brush with more melted butter or margarine, then sprinkle with salt, pepper, nutmeg, and garlic. Repeat until all the potatoes are used. Brush a piece of parchment or baking paper with melted butter or margarine and lay this over the dish.

Place the dish over a medium-hot hot plate for about 4 minutes, to brown the base of the potatoes. Transfer the dish to a preheated oven and cook at 375°F (190°C) for 35 minutes, or until the potatoes feel tender when prodded with a sharp knife.

To serve, remove the paper 'lid' and place a warmed serving plate over the dish. Turn smoothly upside-down so that the potato cake is transferred to the plate. Serve at once, cut in wedges like a regular cake.

SERVES 6

PIPED POTATOES WITH ALMONDS

....

POMMES AMANDINE

A mixture of mashed potato, butter, and egg is known as a 'duchess' in culinary parlance. My almond-flavoured duchess mixture is used here as a shell to hold a mixture of vegetables in cream sauce.
When cold, the mixture can be formed into croquettes of any shape, coated in flour, beaten egg, then breadcrumbs, and fried until golden.

ALMOND-FLAVORED DUCHESS

1½ lbs. (750 g) potatoes, peeled and quartered

2 oz. (60 g) butter

3 egg yolks, beaten

sea salt and freshly ground black pepper

½ cup (2 oz., 60 g) ground almonds

FILLING

½ cup (3 oz., 90 g) cooked green peas

½ cup (3 oz., 90 g) corn kernels

½ cup (4 fl. oz., 125 ml) white sauce (see p. 166)

sea salt and freshly ground black pepper

1 cup (4 oz., 125 g) lightly toasted, slivered almonds

Boil the potatoes in salted water for 25 minutes until cooked. Drain.

Reheat the potatoes very gently for 4 minutes to dry them out, then sieve or mash thoroughly to form a smooth purée. Return to the saucepan with the butter and warm through.

Stir in the egg yolks, salt, and pepper to mix well, then add the almonds.

Put the duchess mixture into a pastry bag with a fluted tip (nozzle). On a greased baking sheet (tray), pipe potato 'nests': start from the center and pipe out in a spiral to make the base, then pipe a ring on top, around the edge, to make a little wall. Make 8 nests. Dry under the broiler (griller) for a few minutes but do not allow to color too much.

In a saucepan, prepare the filling. Blend the peas, corn, and white sauce together and season to taste with salt and pepper.

Fill the potato nests with this mixture and sprinkle with almonds. Bake at 400°F (200°C) for 4 minutes and serve hot.

Note: The potato shells can be brushed with beaten egg for a better color, or melted butter for extra flavor.

SERVES 4

TWO TYPES OF BEAN IN A RICH DRESSING

....

LES HARICOTS PANACHÉS TARBAISE

Beans were one of the finest cultivated crops. Some varieties were being grown in the area of Switzerland and northern Italy as early as the Bronze Age, and the Ancient Egyptians took them as an emblem for life itself. Flageolets are the finest, most delicious of all the dried varieties of beans, while tiny French beans are the best fresh type. These two types of beans are often served together in France, the pods and the seeds providing an interesting contrast of texture, flavor, and color.

1 cup (8 oz., 250 g) flageolet beans, soaked overnight in distilled or boiled water, washed, and drained

1 onion, studded with 2 cloves

½ carrot

sprig of thyme

8 oz. (250 g) fresh, small French beans

DRESSING

⅓ cup (2 oz., 60 g) chopped onion

1 teaspoon Dijon mustard

1 egg, hard-boiled, shelled, and chopped

3 tablespoons white wine vinegar

3 tablespoons walnut oil

3 tablespoons plain yogurt

sea salt and freshly ground black pepper

1 tablespoon chopped fresh chives

1 clove garlic, chopped

juice and finely grated rind of 1 lemon

2 tablespoons chopped fresh parsley

Cook the flageolet beans in a saucepan full of water, covered with a lid, so that they are just simmering gently at all times. Skim off any scum that rises to the surface.

After 2 hours — by which time the flageolets should be nearly cooked — add the onion, carrot, and thyme. Cook for a further 30 minutes, until the flageolets are done. Drain the flageolets, place in a serving bowl, and keep hot.

Boil the French beans in salted water for 6 to 8 minutes, then drain. Place in the serving bowl with the flageolets.

Put all the dressing ingredients into a blender or food processor and blend together.

Toss the hot beans in the cold dressing and serve immediately.

SERVES 4

POTATOES WITH A CREAMY HERB SAUCE

RAGOÛT DE POMMES À L'ORIGAN

This simple side dish is rich without being heavy, and piquant without swamping the food it accompanies.

2 lbs. (1 kg) new potatoes

2 tablespoons (1 oz., 30 g) butter

¼ cup (1 oz., 30 g) whole-wheat (wholemeal) flour

scant 2 cups (15 fl. oz., 475 ml) milk

1 teaspoon chopped fresh oregano

1 teaspoon chopped fresh coriander

sea salt and freshly ground black pepper

3 tablespoons sour cream

⅓ cup (3 fl. oz., 90 ml) plain yogurt

1 tablespoon chopped fresh parsley, to garnish

Boil the potatoes in salted water for 20 minutes, or until tender. Drain and set aside.

Heat the butter in a large pan and add the flour, stirring to make a roux. Cook this for 2 minutes without allowing to brown, then add the milk gradually, stirring all the while, to make a smooth white sauce.

Stir in the oregano and coriander, and season to taste with salt and pepper.

Peel and thickly slice the potatoes when cool enough to handle. Stir gently into the sauce. Simmer for 3 minutes.

Just before serving, stir in the sour cream and yogurt. Spoon into a warmed serving dish, sprinkle with parsley, and serve at once.

SERVES 6

LEEKS IN A HONEY SAUCE

POIREAUX CONFITS AU MIEL CÔTE D'AZUR

The perfume industry of France is centered around the little town of Grasse in southern France, where the fields are full of lavender and other flowers. The bees there make a honey that is richly scented and flavored with their meadow harvest.

12 small leeks, trimmed and cleaned well

2 oz. (60 g) butter

2 tablespoons French or other honey

juice of 1 lemon

1 tablespoon white wine vinegar

⅔ cup (5 fl. oz., 155 ml) sweet white wine

sea salt and freshly ground black pepper

Tie the leeks in bundles of six and boil in salted water for 12 minutes. Drain well and gently squeeze out any excess moisture. Place in an ovenproof dish and set aside.

Melt the butter in a saucepan. Stir in the honey and cook gently for about 15 minutes to make a rich caramel. Stir in the lemon juice, vinegar, and wine, bring to the boil, and cook for 4 minutes more. Season to taste with salt and pepper.

Pour the sauce over the leeks and cook in a preheated oven at 400°F (200°C) for 15 minutes. Serve at once.

SERVES 4

Pictured opposite: Potatoes with a Creamy Herb Sauce, and Leeks in a Honey Sauce

BRAISED BELGIAN ENDIVE IN A WATERCRESS AND RADISH SAUCE

....

ENDIVE BRAISÉES, SAUCE CRESSON

Braised Belgian endive (chicory) is a traditional dish in the Flemish-influenced regions of northern France. In this recipe it is served with a modern watercress sauce.

SAUCE CRESSON
2 bunches watercress, coarse stems and leaves discarded
6 radishes, cleaned and sliced
1 slice preserved ginger
¼ cup (2 fl. oz., 60 ml) sunflower oil
8 oz. (250 g) silken tofu
sea salt and freshly ground black pepper
juice of 1 lemon

FOR THE BELGIAN ENDIVE
8 heads Belgian endive (chicory), trimmed and discolored end and outer leaves discarded
juice of 1 orange and 1 lemon
1 teaspoon honey
freshly ground black pepper

Reserve a few nice sprigs of watercress for the garnish. Place the remaining watercress in a blender or food processor with the radishes, ginger, oil, and tofu. Blend to a smooth cream, then season with salt and pepper and stir in the lemon juice. Set aside.

Place the Belgian endive in a baking dish. Stir together the orange and lemon juice, honey, and pepper. Pour this over the endive.

Cover the dish with a lid or aluminum foil and bake in an oven preheated at 400°F (200°C) for about 35 minutes.

To serve, drain the Belgian endive and place on a warmed serving dish. Drizzle the sauce over and garnish with sprigs of watercress.

Note: The heads of Belgian endive can be browned in a little oil in a saucepan before they are braised.

SERVES 4

LETTUCES GLAZED WITH A CIDER SAUCE

....

LAITUES GLACÉES SAINT QUENTIN

Many members of my family have been professional caterers, some in five-star restaurants, some in modest bistros. This dish comes from the Restaurant de la Gare at Roisel, near Saint Quentin, which was run by my Uncle Robert and his wife Marguerite, who was one of the best cooks in our family. This light lettuce dish was her specialty, made from lettuces grown in her own large garden.

2 tablespoons (1 oz., 30 g) butter
2 shallots, chopped
1 large apple, cored and sliced
½ cup (4 fl. oz., 125 ml) dry cider
sea salt and freshly ground black pepper
6 soft lettuces with firm hearts, wilted leaves discarded, trimmed of stem ends, washed, and drained
½ cup (4 fl. oz., 125 ml) heavy cream *or* plain yogurt
3 egg yolks

Heat the butter in a saucepan and sauté the shallots for 2 minutes, then add the apple and cook for a further 4 minutes. Stir in the cider and simmer gently for 10 minutes until the apple is reduced to a thick purée. Set aside to cool slightly.

Meanwhile, bring a pan of salted water to the boil and cook the lettuces for 8 minutes. Drain well and squeeze gently to remove excess water. Cool slightly before folding the lettuces into neat parcels and arranging in the base of a shallow ovenproof dish.

Season the sauce with salt and pepper, stir in the yogurt or cream, then beat in the egg yolks. Pour over the lettuce.

Place the dish in an oven preheated at 475°F (240°C) for 10 minutes to thicken and glaze the sauce. Remove from the oven and serve at once.

SERVES 6

Pictured opposite: Peas Cooked with Button Onions and Lettuce in Butter

Peas Cooked with Button Onions and Lettuce in Butter

Les Petits Pois à la Française

I think it is the color that puts many people off the traditional French way of cooking peas — and for those who expect peas to be vivid green bullets, a first glimpse of this dish will come as something of a shock.
The yellowy-brown color change that the peas undergo in such dishes comes with longer, slower cooking and is accompanied by a wonderful development of flavor — ask any French gourmet.
Although usually eaten as a side dish, this one is often served as a course on its own in France, and makes a tasty supper dish, accompanied by a baked potato.

4 oz. (125 g) butter
12 button onions, peeled and rinsed
1 small crisphead lettuce, leaves separated and torn
2 lbs. (1 kg) freshly picked green peas, shelled, washed, and drained
1 teaspoon Demerara (raw) sugar
sea salt and freshly ground black pepper
1 tablespoon whole-wheat (wholemeal) flour

Heat three-quarters of the butter in a small saucepan and sauté the onion for 3 minutes without browning. Add the lettuce and cook for 1 minute, then add the peas. Pour in just enough water to come level with the vegetables. Season with sugar, salt, and pepper. Cook gently for about 15 to 20 minutes, until the vegetables are tender.

In a bowl, blend the remaining butter with the flour to make a paste (this is called *beurre manié*) and stir this into the boiling liquid to thicken. Check the seasoning.

Serve on a large plate, preferably surrounded with a border of baked potatoes.

VARIATIONS
A little freshly chopped mint can be sprinkled over the vegetables.

Blend with 2½ cups (1 imp. pint, 310 ml) milk to make a soup. Alternatively, drain the vegetables and push through a sieve to make a purée for filling artichoke bottoms.

SERVES 4

BRAISED CELERY WITH A YOGURT AND ROQUEFORT SAUCE

CELERI AU YAOURT ET ROQUEFORT

Celery stalks can be used in soups, salads, as crudités, or braised and served hot with a sauce, as in this dish.

5 cups (2 imp. pints, 1.25 litres) water
2 tablespoons white wine vinegar
2 heads celery, trimmed, leaves and damaged stalks
discarded, and cut into 2-in. (5-cm) pieces
2 tablespoons whole-wheat (wholemeal) flour
2 tablespoons vegetable oil
2 oz. (60 g) butter

SAUCE
2 tablespoons (1 oz., 30 g) butter
2 tablespoons whole-wheat (wholemeal) flour
1¼ cups (10 fl. oz., 310 ml) celery stock
sea salt and freshly ground black pepper
freshly grated nutmeg
½ cup (2 oz., 60 g) grated Roquefort cheese
½ cup (4 fl. oz., 125 ml) plain yogurt
3 tablespoons water
1 teaspoon cornstarch (cornflour)

1 tablespoon freshly chopped parsley, to garnish
2 eggs, hard-boiled, shelled, and chopped, to garnish

Put water and vinegar in a saucepan and bring to the boil. Blend the flour and oil together, then stir in. Add the celery and boil for 10 minutes, then refresh in cold water. Reserve 1¼ cups (10 fl. oz., 310 ml) of the celery stock.

Heat the butter in a large saucepan. Pack the celery pieces in the bottom and add water to come just level with the celery. Boil for 35 minutes.

Meanwhile, melt the butter in a saucepan and add the flour. Cook for 3 minutes, stirring continuously, without browning. Gradually stir in the reserved celery stock. When the sauce is thick and smooth, add the salt, pepper, nutmeg, and cheese. Keep hot but do not allow to boil.

In a cup, blend the yogurt and water together with the cornstarch. Pour gradually into the hot sauce and return to boiling point, then simmer gently for 4 minutes. Strain and check seasoning.

Drain the celery. Arrange in a shallow serving dish and pour over the sauce. Sprinkle with parsley and egg and serve immediately.

SERVES 4

GRATIN OF BROCCOLI AND POTATOES

LES BROCOLIS AUX POMMES À LA VENDÉENNE

The Vendée is the province where I was born. Many of the best French country dishes originated in this region. Much of the farmland is of a very high quality, some of the best having been reclaimed from the sea in the 11th century. This has become the market garden of France, producing a wide range of excellent vegetables. Consequently, our version of the traditional gratin includes more than just the standard potato slices. Almost any vegetable could be substituted for the broccoli in this recipe.

8 oz. (250 g) broccoli, trimmed, washed well,
and drained
8 oz. (250 g) potatoes, peeled and sliced
5 cups (2 imp. pints, 1.25 litres) water
3 garlic cloves, chopped

SAUCE
¼ cup (2 oz., 60 g) good-quality butter (preferably
Normandy or Vendée butter)
2 tablespoons whole-wheat (wholemeal) flour
⅔ cup (5 fl. oz., 155 ml) vegetable stock
⅔ cup (5 fl. oz., 155 ml) light cream
1 cup (4 oz., 125 g) grated hard cheese of choice
sea salt and freshly ground black pepper

Put the broccoli in a large saucepan with the potatoes, water, and garlic, and boil until the vegetables are tender but not overcooked.

Drain the vegetables, reserving ⅔ cup (5 fl. oz., 155 ml) of the liquid for the sauce. Place the vegetables in a shallow earthenware baking dish and set aside.

To make the sauce, heat the butter in a saucepan and stir in the flour. Cook gently, stirring to form a roux. Do not allow to brown.

Gradually add the vegetable stock, stirring all the time to make a smooth mixture, then slowly add the cream. Mix in half the cheese and season to taste with salt and pepper.

Cover the vegetables with this sauce, then sprinkle over the remaining cheese. Place under a hot broiler (griller) until sizzling hot and golden-brown. Serve at once.

SERVES 4

Pictured opposite: Braised Celery with a Yogurt and Roquefort Sauce, and Gratin of Broccoli and Potatoes

FENNEL AND TOMATO BAKE

....

FENOUIL À LA CONFITURE DE TOMATE

Fennel's pungent aniseed taste is mellowed by cooking, and is well matched in this piquant bake with tomatoes, raspberry vinegar, and honey. To turn this dish into a meal, lay poached eggs over the finished dish and drizzle with a classic French 'beurre blanc' (see p. 166).

**4 large bulbs fennel, trimmed, split down the middle,
and washed well
1 tablespoon olive oil
4 large beefsteak tomatoes, skinned, deseeded,
and chopped
1 tablespoon clear honey
1 tablespoon raspberry vinegar
4 basil leaves, chopped
sea salt and freshly ground black pepper**

Bring a large pan of salted water to the boil and cook the fennel for 20 minutes.

Refresh the fennel in cold water, then lay in a shallow earthenware baking dish. Brush with oil.

Scatter the tomatoes over the fennel.

Mix together the honey and vinegar and drizzle over the dish. Sprinkle with basil, salt, and pepper.

Place the dish in an oven preheated at 400°F (200°C) and bake for 12 to 15 minutes so that the tomatoes cook to a rich sauce over the fennel. Serve immediately.

If you wish to make it a main meal, serve as described above with poached eggs and a white butter sauce.

SERVES 4

THREE TYPES OF WILD MUSHROOM IN A WINE, CREAM, AND SAFFRON SAUCE

....

LES TROIS SAUVAGES

Dried mushrooms can be bought in many delicatessens and health shops. They must be soaked for an hour to restore them to their original size. In this dish I have used cèpes, morels (a spongy variety), and English field mushrooms, but other varieties could be used.

**1/4 cup (2 oz., 60 g) mixed oil and butter
1 small onion, chopped, *or* 3 shallots, chopped
1 small garlic clove, chopped
1 teaspoon whole-wheat (wholemeal) flour
2 tablespoons white port *or* white wine
large pinch of ground saffron
sea salt and freshly ground black pepper
small pinch of thyme
pinch each of paprika and turmeric
1/2 cup (4 fl. oz., 125 ml) light cream
extra 2 oz. (60 g) butter
4 oz. (125 g) fresh cèpes, trimmed, wiped, and sliced,
or 1 1/2 oz. (45 g) dried cèpes, soaked for 1 hour
and sliced
4 oz. (125 g) fresh morels, trimmed, wiped, and sliced,
or 1 1/2 oz. (45 g) dried morels, soaked for 1 hour
and sliced
4 oz. (125 g) fresh field mushrooms, trimmed, wiped,
and sliced
16 scallions (spring onions)**

Heat the mixed oil and butter in a saucepan and sauté the onion or shallots and the garlic for 4 minutes without browning. Sprinkle on the flour and stir to absorb the fat. Add the port or wine and the saffron, stirring continuously, then add the salt, pepper, thyme, paprika, and turmeric and cook gently for 5 minutes.

Blend in the cream and cook for a further 5 minutes. Strain the sauce and set aside.

Heat the additional butter in a separate saucepan and cook the three different types of mushroom in turn, for 3 minutes each. Drain and arrange on a serving dish in separate piles.

Tie the scallions in a bundle and boil for 8 minutes. Drain, squeeze gently, and arrange on the serving dish between the piles of mushrooms. Pour a little sauce over each pile.

Serve with toasted whole-wheat (wholemeal) bread or fresh rolls to mop up the juices.

Pictured above right: Mushroom Ratatouille

SERVES 4

MUSHROOM RATATOUILLE

MÉLANGE DES ANGES D'ARMENONVILLE

This is an unusual ratatouille, which I learned while working in a restaurant in the suburbs of Paris. It is primarily made from mushrooms and eggplants (aubergines), and is cooked only briefly, unlike the traditional version. Yet it is one of the best ratatouilles I have ever tasted.

1/4 cup (2 fl. oz., 60 ml) walnut oil
1 large onion, thinly sliced
1 lb. (500 g) eggplant (aubergines), thinly sliced, rinsed in cold running water to remove bitter juices, and drained
1 lb. (500 g) button mushrooms, trimmed and wiped

2/3 cup (5 fl. oz., 155 ml) dry white wine
1/3 cup (3 oz., 90 g) tomato paste (purée)
4 garlic cloves, crushed
2 shallots, chopped
sea salt and freshly ground black pepper
1 tablespoon chopped fresh basil, to garnish

Heat the oil in a large saucepan and sauté the onion for 4 minutes. Add the eggplant slices and sauté for 5 minutes until tender.

Add the mushrooms to the saucepan along with the wine. Bring to the boil and simmer for 5 minutes. Stir in the tomato paste, garlic, and shallots. Cover and simmer for 15 minutes.

Season the ratatouille to taste with salt and pepper. Sprinkle with the basil just before serving.

SERVES 6

Warm and Cold Salads

Les Salades Chaudes et Froides

Orange and Spinach Salad with Roquefort Dressing

La Salade Ronsard

Pierre Ronsard was the youngest son of the maître d'hotel of King Francis I. The 'Prince of Poets', as Ronsard was known, wrote a poem called 'La Salade', in which he used this food as a model for the simple life, contrasting the natural healthfulness of country life with the pomp and artifice of the Court.

DRESSING
2 tablespoons rosé wine

2 tablespoons walnut oil

juice and grated rind of 1 orange

1/2 cup (2 oz., 60 g) crumbled Roquefort cheese

1 tablespoon chopped fresh chervil

sea salt and freshly ground black pepper

SALAD
oil, for frying

1 garlic clove, flattened

6 thick slices whole-wheat (wholemeal) bread, crusts discarded, cut into cubes

1 lb. (500 g) young spinach leaves, roughly torn and tough stems discarded

3 oranges, peeled and segmented

2 cups (4 oz., 125 g) sliced mushrooms

Put the dressing ingredients in a blender or food processor and blend until smooth. Set aside.

Pour oil into a skillet or frying pan to a depth of about ½ in. (1 cm), add the garlic, and heat gently. When the garlic is sizzling, add the cubes of bread, a few at a time, and fry until golden, tossing the pan so that the cubes cook evenly.

Remove the croutons with a slotted spoon and drain on paper towels.

Place the spinach in a large bowl. Add the orange segments and mushrooms.

Toss with a little of the dressing, then scatter over the warm croutons. Serve with the remaining dressing offered separately.

VARIATION
Corn salad — also known as mâche or lamb's lettuce — or salad burnet could take the place of all or part of the spinach.

SERVES 4

Pictured on previous pages: Orange and Spinach Salad with Roquefort Dressing, and Brandied Tomato Salad
Pictured opposite: Chickpea and Chicory Salad

Brandied Tomato Salad

La Salade de Tomates au Cognac

Never add a dressing to a tomato salad too far in advance — this applies to lettuce-based salads too. A dressing will draw the juices out of tomatoes, making the salad watery if left too long, and wilt lettuce. Salads based on rice, root vegetables, or pulses often benefit from the dressing being added while the cooked ingredients are still hot, because when a hot ingredient cools in a cold dressing, it soaks up more of the dressing, and the resulting salad is more enjoyable.
It is interesting to note that the more acid-tasting the tomato, the higher the vitamin C content. This vitamin is destroyed by cooking, so a tangy tomato salad is a tasty treat that will boost your vitamin C levels too.

DRESSING
juice of 1 1/2 lemons

grated rind of 1 lemon

juice of 1/2 orange

2 tablespoons walnut oil

1 tablespoon wine vinegar

1/2 cup (4 fl. oz., 125 ml) plain yogurt

1 teaspoon French mustard

1 teaspoon honey

sea salt and freshly ground black pepper

SALAD
2 lbs. (1 kg) tomatoes, sliced horizontally, *or* halved cherry tomatoes

2 oranges, peeled and segmented

1/2 cup (4 fl. oz., 125 ml) brandy

2 tablespoons chopped fresh chives

1 green sweet pepper (capsicum), sliced into rings, to garnish

Put all the dressing ingredients in a blender or food processor and blend to a smooth, creamy texture. Set aside in the refrigerator until needed.

Place the tomato slices on a large, flat serving dish so that they overlap slightly, or put the halved cherry tomatoes in a bowl. Arrange the orange segments around the tomatoes, or toss through the cherry tomatoes. Pour the brandy over and leave to marinate for 10 minutes.

Drain off the brandy without disturbing the salad. Add the brandy to the dressing and shake well to mix.

Pour the dressing over the salad, sprinkle with the chives, and decorate with pepper rings. Serve immediately.

SERVES 4

CHICKPEA AND CHICORY SALAD

LA FRISÉE DE PICARDIE AUX POIS CHICHES

Chicory (endive) has a distinctive, bitter flavor that is pleasantly offset by the creamy, nutty taste of the chickpeas in this appetizing and protein-rich salad.

DRESSING
1 teaspoon Dijon mustard
¼ cup (1 oz., 30 g) chopped walnuts
1 garlic clove, chopped
4 oz. (125 g) silken tofu
1 small shallot, finely chopped
⅓ cup (3 fl. oz., 90 ml) apple juice
1 tablespoon cider vinegar
sea salt and freshly ground black pepper

SALAD
8 oz. (250 g) new potatoes
1 medium can chickpeas (garbanzos)
4 quail eggs (optional)
1 medium chicory (endive), leaves separated, washed, and drained
2 red-skinned apples, cored, quartered, and cut into thin triangles
½ cup (2 oz., 60 g) chopped walnuts
1 tablespoon snipped chives

Put all the dressing ingredients in a blender or food processor and blend until smooth. Set aside for the flavors to mingle and develop.

Boil the new potatoes for 20 minutes in plenty of salted water until tender. Drain.

Heat the chickpeas gently in their liquid. Drain Boil the quail eggs for 6 minutes. Remove shells.

Arrange the chicory leaves on individual plates or a large platter. Place the apples on top.

Slice the potatoes and arrange on the plate, perhaps as a border to the leaves or in a central flower design. Scatter chickpeas and walnuts over, then place a quail's egg on each portion.

Drizzle a little dressing over and scatter with chives. Serve at once, so that the eggs, chickpeas, and potatoes are still warm.

SERVES 4

Meridional Salad
with Olives

La Salade Paul et Rose Cézanne

Paul Cézanne's sister, Rose, married Maxime Conil in 1881, and the great Impressionist painter often visited the Conil estate at Montbriant. Paul and Maxime used to argue, and Cézanne once wrote to Emile Zola that Maxime's only talent was selecting olives for a salad — he was too much of a bon viveur for Paul's liking! In this letter he included some verse about his brother-in-law:

'O fils dégénéré, tu fais ici la noce!
Hélas! Ton habit neuf est tout taché de sauce,
. . . Abjure les liqueurs, c'est trés pernicieux
et ne bois que l'eau, tu t'en trouveras mieux.'
'Oh degenerate son, thou art overly enjoying thyself!
Alas! Your new suit is all stained with sauce,
. . . Forswear all liqueur, it is pernicious
and let water be your only drink, for then you will enjoy good health.'

DRESSING

3 tablespoons olive oil

2 tablespoons wine vinegar

2 oz. (60 g) fresh goat's cheese

1 teaspoon Dijon mustard

sea salt and freshly ground black pepper

SALAD

8 oz. (250 g) green beans

1 head curly endive, leaves separated

12 leaves corn salad (mâche, lamb's lettuce)

6 garlic cloves, finely chopped

2½ cups (5 oz., 155 g) croutons

1¼ cups (5 oz., 155 g) walnuts

1⅔ cups (8 oz., 250 g) mixed green and black olives, pitted

6 eggs, hard-boiled and sliced

3 large beefsteak tomatoes, sliced, *or* 400 g cherry tomatoes, halved

Put all the dressing ingredients in a blender or food processor and blend until smooth.

Blanch the beans in boiling water.

Place the curly endive and corn salad in a large bowl with the beans, garlic, croutons, walnuts, and olives. Toss well, then drizzle with most of the dressing, and toss again.

Place the salad in individual serving bowls or one large bowl and decorate with the egg and tomato. Drizzle the last of the dressing over the slices, then serve at once.

SERVES 4

Avocado and Cucumber
Salad in a Mint Dressing

Avocat et Concombre, Sauce Menthe

This is a deliciously cool salad to refresh you on a hot summer's day.

DRESSING

½ cup (2 oz., 60 g) cucumber skin

6 mint leaves

2 garlic cloves, chopped

3 oz. (90 g) silken tofu

juice of 1 lemon

sea salt and freshly ground black pepper

SALAD

2 ripe avocados, halved, pitted, peeled, and sliced

1 cucumber, peeled and sliced

1 head curly endive, leaves separated

Put the dressing ingredients in a blender or food processor and blend to a smooth cream. Adjust the consistency with a little water if too thick.

Place the curly endive leaves on a serving plate. Arrange the avocado and cucumber on top.

Drizzle an attractive ribbon of dressing over the salad and serve.

VARIATION

The dressing could be spooned onto individual plates in a little pool before the slices of avocado and cucumber are arranged over it. Garnish with fronds of curly endive.

SERVES 4

Pictured opposite: Meridional Salad with Olives, and Avocado and Cucumber Salad in a Mint Dressing

PASTA SALAD WITH FENNEL

LA SALADE DE NOUILLE AU FENOUIL

Pasta makes an excellent and substantial salad dish. Choose whole-wheat (wholemeal) pasta for a dish rich in protein and fiber, although green pasta — if made with spinach and not food dye — is very good for you too, and looks charming.

DRESSING

¼ cup (2 fl. oz., 60 ml) raspberry vinegar

3 oz. (90 g) silken tofu

¼ cup (1 oz., 30 g) slivered almonds

1 teaspoon Dijon mustard

1 teaspoon clear honey

1 tablespoon hot water

sea salt and freshly ground black pepper

SALAD

8 oz. (250 g) thin noodles

1 small oakleaf lettuce, washed and drained

1 small corn salad (mâche, lamb's lettuce), washed and drained

¼ cup (2 fl. oz., 60 ml) vegetable oil

1 small onion, chopped

1 cup (4 oz., 125 g) button mushrooms, thinly sliced

½ cup (2 oz., 60 g) grated Gruyère cheese

sea salt and freshly ground black pepper

1 small head fennel, thinly sliced, to garnish

Put all the dressing ingredients in a blender or food processor and blend to a smooth cream. Check seasoning and set aside for the flavors to develop and mingle.

To make the salad, bring a large saucepan of water to the boil and add the noodles. Simmer for 10 minutes (less if the noodles are fresh) or until the noodles are *al dente*. Drain.

Arrange the lettuce leaves around the edge of four serving plates.

Heat the oil in a saucepan and sauté the onion gently for 3 minutes. Add the mushrooms and cook briefly until they just start to soften.

Add the noodles. Sprinkle with the cheese and salt and pepper. Toss so that the noodles are mixed well with the vegetables and cheese.

Pile the noodles and vegetables into the center of each plate and garnish with the fennel. Serve, with the dressing offered separately.

SERVES 4

RICH RICE SALAD WITH ARTICHOKES AND NASTURTIUM FLOWERS

LA SALADE EDMOND ROSTAND

*Rostand's poignant hero, Cyrano de Bergerac, epitomized the bravado inherent in all Frenchmen. In recent years he has become known as the owner of a somewhat oversized nose, but when the play featuring this great character is staged, it is hailed by the critics. And the ladies? Well, they still fall for Cyrano because, as any Frenchman will tell you, it is poetry that wins genuine affection, not a handsome face.
But equally French is the understanding of food as an aperitif to love. So this splendid salad is named for the creator of the noble Cyrano. In the name of love, you may omit the garlic!*

DRESSING

juice of 1 lemon

1 tablespoon white wine vinegar

2 tablespoons tomato paste (purée)

⅓ cup (3 fl. oz., 90 ml) buttermilk

½ cup (2 oz., 60 g) slivered almonds

1 shallot, finely chopped

1 garlic clove (optional)

sea salt and freshly ground black pepper

SALAD

1 cup (7 oz., 220 g) rice, cooked

4 large crisp lettuce leaves, washed and drained

6 artichoke bottoms, cooked and diced

12 seedless green grapes

chopped fresh coriander *or* chervil, to garnish

nasturtium flowers, to garnish

Put all the dressing ingredients in a blender or food processor and blend to produce an almond-flavored dressing.

Toss the rice in half the dressing. Lay a lettuce leaf on each of four small salad plates, then spoon a little of the rice onto each.

Arrange artichokes and grapes over each portion, then sprinkle with the garnishes. Serve the remaining dressing separately.

VARIATION

For a more substantial salad, add chopped, hard-boiled egg to the finished dish.

SERVES 4

Pictured opposite: Bulghur Wheat Salad with Tomatoes and Olives

BULGHUR WHEAT SALAD WITH TOMATOES AND OLIVES

···

LA TABOULÉE DES CROISADES

Ever since the days of the Crusades, when French and English monarchs were constantly engaged in battles in the Middle East, there have been close links between France and the Arab world — not always so warlike, fortunately. From this, France has absorbed and adapted many dishes, taboulée being but one. Bulghur wheat, also known as burghul, is a coarsely ground wheat that has been partially cooked and then dried. This method was developed in countries where raw grain would otherwise be eaten by insects before it could be prepared for the table.

DRESSING
juice and grated rind of 2 lemons
¹/₃ cup (3 fl oz., 90 ml) olive oil
2 garlic cloves, peeled
10 walnuts, shelled
¹/₄ cup (2 fl. oz., 60 ml) plain yogurt
sea salt and freshly ground black pepper

SALAD
¹/₄ cup (2 fl. oz., 60 ml) mixed butter and olive oil
1 medium onion, chopped

1¹/₃ cups (8 oz., 250 g) bulghur wheat (burghul)
3 cups (24 fl. oz., 750 ml) water
sea salt and freshly ground black pepper
²/₃ cup (4 oz., 125 g) baked beans
4 medium tomatoes, sliced
8 black olives
1 romaine (cos) lettuce, leaves separated, rinsed thoroughly, and drained (if desired, refrigerate briefly to make extra crisp)

Put all the dressing ingredients in a blender or food processor and blend to a smooth cream. Pour into a bottle and refrigerate until needed.

To make the salad, heat the butter and oil in a large saucepan and sauté the onion until translucent but not brown. Add the bulghur wheat and stir for about 5 minutes to coat all the grains with fat. Add the water and boil for 15 to 20 minutes, stirring occasionally. Drain and allow to cool. Season.

Stir in the dressing and the baked beans.

Turn the *taboulée* out into a shallow bowl. Decorate the top with tomato slices and olives. Arrange the leaves around the edge of the bowl or serve separately. Alternatively, spread the leaves out on a serving plate and top with small mounds of *taboulée*. Either way, the leaves are used to scoop up the salad.

SERVES 4

POTATO AND WATERCRESS SALAD FROM AUVERGNE

LA SALADE AUVERGNATE

In terms of flavor, watercress has become a great favorite with the new generation of chefs. Blended with mayonnaise, white sauce, or yogurt, it adds a very special flavor, as well as a most attractive color. We older cooks are inclined to prefer using it raw, its leaves mingling attractively with the other ingredients, as in this salad from Auvergne. The Auvergne is famous for its Cantal cheese, which is featured here in a more substantial salad with new potatoes. The watercress adds color to its pale, creamy-yellow hues. It is best to peel the potatoes, as they will absorb the dressing much better through their flesh than through their skins.

DRESSING

2 tablespoons wine vinegar

¼ cup (2 fl. oz., 60 ml) walnut oil

1 teaspoon Dijon mustard

2 small shallots, chopped

6 watercress leaves

sea salt and freshly ground black pepper

SALAD

1½ lbs. (750 g) new potatoes, washed

1 small bunch watercress, cleaned and tough stalks discarded

5 oz. (155 g) Cantal cheese, cut into ¼-in. (6-mm) cubes

Put all the dressing ingredients in a blender or food processor and blend. Set aside to allow the flavors to mingle and develop.

Boil the potatoes for 20 to 25 minutes, until tender. As soon as they are cool enough to handle, peel and dice, and place in a salad bowl.

Stir the watercress in with the potatoes, add the cheese, and mix together well.

Pour in the dressing and toss to coat everything evenly. Serve.

Note: New potatoes will absorb the dressing best while still warm, and the salad is best served while the potatoes are warm, too, contrasting with the other cold ingredients.

SERVES 4

Pictured opposite: Potato and Watercress Salad from Auvergne, and Flemish Red Cabbage Salad

FLEMISH RED CABBAGE SALAD

LA SALADE FLAMANDE AUX CHOUX ROUGES

A sauerkraut of cabbage — that is, a fermented mixture of red or white cabbage — is very popular in Europe, particularly in its eastern regions. This salad uses red cabbage, but you might like to substitute white cabbage for a more traditional sauerkraut-type base. If you use white cabbage, you may prefer to use a cheese that is milder than a blue cheese — Cheddar, Cantal, Edam, Port Salut, Gouda, or Feta cheese would all be good. Some people find that cabbage has an untoward effect upon their digestive systems — they will be delighted to know that grated carrot is used in almost all coleslaw recipes to combat just this. And marinating the cabbage in the dressing for at least an hour will diminish the inconvenience too.

DRESSING

3 tablespoons cider vinegar

3 tablespoons peanut *or* sunflower oil

1 medium onion, chopped

2 garlic cloves, peeled

2 oz. (60 g) Roquefort cheese or other blue cheese of choice, crumbled

1 teaspoon grainy mustard

1 tablespoon honey

sea salt and freshly ground black pepper

SALAD

1 small red cabbage (about 1 lb., 500 g), quartered, core discarded, and finely sliced

2 large carrots, peeled and grated

4 oz. (125 g) firm blue cheese, cut into small cubes

2 Golden Delicious apples

2 tablespoons chopped fresh parsley

2 tablespoons chopped fresh chives *or* scallions (spring onions)

Put all the dressing ingredients in a blender or food processor and blend for a few seconds until emulsified and thin. Set aside for the flavors to mingle and develop.

Lightly mix the cabbage and carrot in a salad bowl. Stir in the cheese. Toss with the dressing and leave to marinate for 1 hour.

Just before serving, cut the apples into quarters, then cut each quarter across in triangles. Toss with the salad and sprinkle with the parsley and chives or scallions. Serve at once.

SERVES 4

CANTAL CHEESE SALAD

LA SALADE AU FROMAGE DU CANTAL

Many cheeses are used to complement green salads,
either as part of the dressing (blue cheese is well known
in this context) or the garnish. Either way, the result is a
delicious meal or accompanying dish. In France, the
main course is usually followed by a salad then the
cheese plate, before dessert, so this particular salad
combines the two courses into one.

Cantal is a hard, pressed French cheese, which, when
fresh, can have a crumbly texture like that of a mature
English Cheddar or Wensleydale cheese, or Greek Feta.

DRESSING
3 tablespoons cider vinegar
2 tablespoons walnut *or* olive oil
1/2 teaspoon sea salt
freshly ground black pepper
1/2 onion, chopped
1 garlic clove, peeled
1 wedge lemon
1 large sprig parsley, washed and dried
2 tablespoons crumbled Cantal cheese

SALAD
1 lettuce with a firm heart, leaves separated, washed,
and drained

1 red and 1 green sweet pepper (capsicum), deseeded
and chopped
1 tomato, sliced
1 small onion, sliced into rings
1/4 cucumber, sliced
12 black olives
4 oz. (125 g) Cantal, Feta, *or* mature Cheddar cheese,
cut into 1/4-in. (6-mm) cubes
1 tablespoon whole fresh flat (Italian)
parsley leaves

Put all the dressing ingredients into a blender or
food processor (including the lemon wedge,
rind and all) and blend. Do this some time in
advance so the flavors have a chance to mingle.

Put the lettuce leaves and the diced peppers
together in a large salad bowl (preferably a
wooden one). Shake the dressing well before
sprinkling half onto the lettuce and peppers. Toss.

Make a well in the center. Around the top,
arrange a decorative alternating pattern of
tomatoes, onions, cucumbers, and olives.

Place the cheese in the center of the salad and
splash the rest of the dressing over.

Garnish with the parsley leaves and serve
immediately, either as a main course or as the last
course of a meal. Serve with crusty whole-wheat
(wholemeal) bread to mop up the dressing.

SERVES 4

WARM AND
COLD SALADS

FAVA BEAN SALAD WITH FENNEL

LA SALADE DE FÈVES DES MARAIS

Fava (broad) beans make a most delicious salad, especially when they are very young. If you are unsure of the age of the beans, shell them and cook them as described below, but bite one before continuing with the salad. If the skin is tough, as is often the case with older beans, it really is worth removing it. This is no real hardship for four portions and your salad will be the better for it.

Fennel is delicious eaten raw, but for this salad you may wish to boil the slices for 5 minutes first. This is best if your head of fennel seems a tough one, and also if you are unsure whether your guests like this vegetable's distinctive aniseed taste, as this is diminished by boiling.

DRESSING

1 medium onion, chopped

1 tablespoon each fresh chopped savory, tarragon, and parsley

1 teaspoon Dijon mustard

2 tablespoons peanut oil

2 tablespoons cider vinegar

juice and grated rind of 1 lemon

1/2 cup (4 fl. oz., 125 ml) sour cream

1 tablespoon honey

sea salt and freshly ground black pepper

SALAD

2 lbs. (1 kg) fava (broad) beans, shelled

1/2 cup (3 oz., 90 g) canned corn kernels, drained

2 heads fennel, sliced into julienne

4 tomatoes, skinned, deseeded, and chopped

1 tablespoon fresh chopped parsley

Put all the dressing ingredients into a blender or food processor and blend to a smooth cream. Refrigerate until needed.

To prepare the salad, boil the fava beans in lightly salted water for 20 minutes, until tender. Drain, and remove their skins if necessary.

Place the beans, corn, and fennel in a large salad bowl. Stir in the dressing and leave for 1 hour.

Just before serving, top the salad with the chopped tomato and sprinkle with parsley.

VARIATION

Add cooked whole-wheat (wholemeal) pasta shells or macaroni for a nourishing main course salad.

SERVES 4

HAZELNUT SALAD

LA SALADE NOISETIÈRE

My grandmother Mathilde used to make this salad. She'd send us children out to gather dandelion leaves from the meadows around the house, large, white Bigarreaux cherries from the tree in the garden, and hazelnuts from the local woods. The toasted hazelnuts needed for this recipe can be easily bought at the store, but if you have a supply of raw hazelnut kernels, simply toast them in a dry, heavy-based pan for 3 minutes until evenly browned.

DRESSING

1/4 cup (1 oz., 30 g) toasted hazelnuts

1/3 cup (3 fl. oz., 90 ml) buttermilk

1/4 cup (2 fl. oz., 60 ml) sherry vinegar

1 teaspoon Dijon mustard

1 teaspoon clear honey

sea salt and freshly ground black pepper

SALAD

1 crisphead or iceberg lettuce heart, leaves separated, washed, and drained

6 scallions (spring onions), finely sliced

1 small white radish, peeled and finely sliced

2 cups (8 oz., 250 g) white cherries, pitted

1 1/2 cups (8 oz., 250 g) toasted hazelnuts

Put all the dressing ingredients in a blender or food processor and blend to a smooth cream. Set aside for the flavors to develop and mingle.

Arrange the lettuce leaves on individual serving plates. Scatter the scallions and radish over the lettuce or arrange in an attractive mound in the center of each plate.

Decorate with the cherries. Scatter over the hazelnuts and serve at once, offering dressing separately for everyone to serve themselves.

SERVES 4

Pictured opposite: Cantal Cheese Salad

Cheese Dishes
Les Friandises de Fromage

CAMEMBERT CAKES

LES GALETTES FÉCAMPOISE

Camembert was perfected by a Madame Harel in 1790, during the French Revolution. This soft cheese is fermented by the bacillus Camembertii and, when coagulated, it is pressed at a temperature of 64°F (18°C) into the familiar rounds or semi-circles that are synonymous with French cheese for many people.

As with Brie, there are many different types of Camembert. Camembert Fermier, made on the farm, is quite a rarity, even in France, but is worth seeking out as it is more rich and fruity in flavor than the more common, commercially produced Camembert. Another type is Camembert Affiné, which develops an orangy skin as the cheese gets really ripe. This is for cheese fans only as it gets very smelly at this stage too!

These little Camembert Cakes from Normandy make a delicious lunch dish with a crisp salad and a bottle of chilled Normandy cider.

4 oz. (125 g) butter, softened
8 oz. (250 g) medium-ripe Camembert
3 eggs, beaten
4 cups (1 lb., 500 g) self-rising whole-wheat (wholemeal) flour
sea salt
pinch of cayenne pepper
1/2 teaspoon cumin seeds
1 egg yolk
2 tablespoons water

Cream the butter and cheese together to a smooth paste.

Stir in the beaten eggs and the flour a little at a time, then add the salt, cayenne pepper, and cumin seeds. The paste should be the consistency of shortcrust pastry. Roll into a ball and allow to stand for an hour or two.

Dust a pastry board with flour. Divide the dough into small pieces, each about the size of an egg. Roll them out on the board into rounds ¼ in. (6 mm) thick.

Place the rounds on a greased baking sheet (tray) and brush with a wash made from the egg yolk and water. Bake in a preheated oven at 400°F (200°C) for 15 to 20 minutes.

Serve immediately.

SERVES 8

CHOUX PASTRY WITH CHEESE

LA GOUGÈRE BOURGUIGNONNE

Once mastered, the technique of making choux pastry is very easy and, like a soufflé, it always impresses your guests. Having tried it, I think you will find it so simple and so delicious that you will not want to save it for special occasions.

A gougère makes a tasty light meal at any time of the day — best enjoyed with a glass of Chablis.

2 quantities choux pastry (see p. 159)
pinch of celery seeds
4 oz. (125 g) Gruyère cheese, half of quantity grated, the remainder cut into small cubes
extra 2 tablespoons (1 oz., 30 g) butter
extra 1 tablespoon whole-wheat (wholemeal) flour

For the choux pastry, put the water, butter, and salt (quantities on p. 159) in a saucepan and heat to boiling point. When the buttery water boils, tip in all the flour at once, very quickly, and stir fast to blend together. Keep stirring over the heat until the mixture forms a smooth, very thick paste that comes away cleanly from the sides of the pan in a solid mass. Remove from the heat and allow to cool for 4 minutes.

Add the eggs to the paste a little at a time, making sure they are well blended. Stop adding egg when the mixture is of a very thick but pourable consistency — 'holding a thread' is the culinary term.

Add some freshly ground pepper and the celery seeds. Stir the grated cheese into the mixture, then the cubes of cheese, making sure the cubes are evenly distributed.

Grease a ring or savarin mold with the extra butter, then sprinkle with the extra flour. Pour the mixture into this mold.

Bake on the middle shelf of a preheated oven at 400°F (200°C) for 30 to 35 minutes. Turn out onto a flat dish, cut into portions, and serve.

VARIATIONS

Most hard cheeses, whether English or French, can be used for this dish.

Almonds or aniseed can be sprinkled over the top of the mixture before baking.

The dish looks even more attractive baked in individual ring molds.

MAKES A 1-LB. (500-G) GOUGÈRE

Pictured on previous pages: Camembert Cakes
Pictured opposite: Soup with Cheese

SOUP WITH CHEESE

LA SOUPE AU FROMAGE

Many cheeses are excellent sources of protein, vitamins, and minerals — about 2 oz. (60 g) of Cheddar or Parmesan cheese contains the recommended daily intake of calcium for an adult. Cheese is, however, high in fat, which means it is high in calories, and that fat is saturated, which means high cholesterol. However, a light soup such as this can counterbalance this excess and still be delicious, satisfying, and wholesome.

4 oz. (125 g) butter
1 onion, sliced
2 carrots, peeled and sliced
8 oz. (250 g) potatoes, peeled and sliced
5 cups (2 imp. pints, 1.25 litres) water
2½ cups (1 imp. pint, 625 ml) milk
sea salt and freshly ground black pepper
freshly ground nutmeg
8 slices whole-wheat (wholemeal) bread
8 slices Cheddar *or* Gruyère cheese

Heat the butter in a large saucepan and sauté the onion, carrots, and potatoes for about 6 minutes but do not allow to brown. Add the water and boil for 20 minutes.

Remove the vegetables and blend in a blender or food processor with a little of the cooking liquid. Stir back into the rest of the cooking liquid to form a thin purée.

Add the milk and reheat. Season to taste with salt, pepper, and nutmeg.

Toast the bread. Lay a slice of cheese on each slice of toast and place under a broiler (griller) to melt the cheese. Put one piece of cheese toast in each bowl and pour the soup over it, allowing the bread to absorb a little soup.

Note: The character of this soup is modified according to the cheese used. The best English cheese, other than Cheddar, is double Gloucester; the best French cheeses are Cantal and Port Salut. Dutch Gouda and Edam have the necessary melting qualities, and Edam is low in fat, too.

SERVES 8

103
CHEESE
DISHES

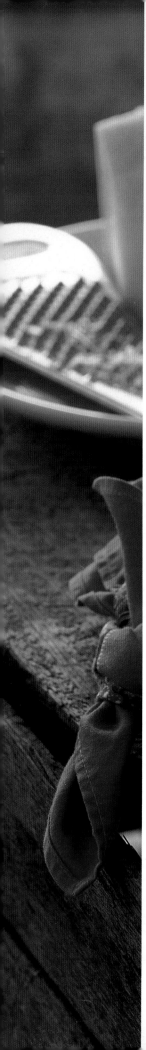

CLASSIC CHEESE SOUFFLÉ

SOUFFLÉ AU FROMAGE

It is sad that the soufflé has a mystique that makes many people scared to try making one. Provided the instructions are followed carefully, it is very hard to go wrong with a soufflé, and the effect is magical and delicious. This is a great quick dish but, for beginners, preparation may be easier with two pairs of hands. Here's hoping you have a willing assistant.

1 oz. (30 g) butter

1 cup (4 oz., 125 g) whole-wheat (wholemeal) flour

2½ cups (1 imp. pint, 625 ml) milk

5 oz. (155 g) Gruyère cheese, grated

sea salt and freshly ground black pepper

pinch of grated nutmeg

5 eggs, separated

extra pinch of salt

1 extra egg white (optional)

¼ cup (1 oz., 30 g) freshly grated Parmesan cheese (optional)

In a large, heavy-based saucepan, heat the butter until sizzling, then stir in the flour. Cook, stirring all the time, until you have a very thick roux. Add the milk a very little at a time, stirring to blend completely between each addition. You should end up with a very thick sauce. Add the cheese and stir to amalgamate well. Keep cooking gently, stirring all the time, until the cheese has melted. Season with salt, pepper, and nutmeg and remove from the heat.

Beat the egg yolks into the sauce until completely blended.

Whisk the egg whites (the optional extra egg white will give extra lift) with a pinch of salt in a clean bowl until very stiff. Using a metal spoon, fold one large spoonful into the cheese sauce to 'loosen' it, then carefully fold the remaining egg white in, a bit at a time. Do not overblend — a few clumps of white in the mixture are all right; it is more important not to burst all the air bubbles.

Pour the mixture into a lightly oiled soufflé dish (about 1½-quart (2½-imp. pint, 1.5-litre) capacity). If you wish, you can sprinkle the interior of the dish with grated Parmesan cheese first. Run a finger around the top of the dish to form a little trough between it and the mixture. This helps the soufflé to rise evenly.

Bake in the center of a preheated oven at 350°F (180°C) for 45 minutes. It should be well-risen and golden on top, while the center should be very slightly soft or runny. Serve immediately.

SERVES 4

LITTLE TARTLETS FILLED WITH A BRIE CHEESE SOUFFLÉ

LES TALMOUSES DE SAINT-DENIS AU BRIE

This is one of the oldest French cheese pastries, dating from the 12th century. The tartlets were created by the people of Sarcelles, who presented them to the Archbishop of Paris accompanied by this little poem:

'Des Talmouses de Saint-Denis,
Vous vous portez fort bien aussi,
Comme on voit à votre frimousse,
Qu'on prendrait pour une Talmouse.'
'The Talmouses of Saint-Denis
Keep you in very good health
As one can see from your round, shiny face
Which one would take for a Talmouse.'

There is a modern version of this dish, which uses chopped cheese blended with choux pastry as a filling for a pastry case. I prefer the old-fashioned Talmouse, and it is this recipe that I give you now.

8 oz. (250 g) Brie cheese, rind cut off

8 oz. (250 g) cream cheese

sea salt and freshly ground black pepper

freshly grated nutmeg

2 teaspoons Demerara (raw) sugar

1 tablespoon cornstarch (cornflour)

4 egg yolks

2 egg whites

1 lb. (500 g) shop-bought puff pastry *or* 1½ quantities puff pastry (see p. 159)

Pound the Brie to a smooth paste along with the cream cheese. Season with salt, pepper, nutmeg, and sugar.

Blend the cornstarch into the cheese, followed by the egg yolks, to make an evenly mixed, smooth cream.

In a separate bowl, whisk the egg whites until they form firm peaks, then gradually fold into the cheese mixture.

Roll out the puff pastry and use it to line 24 tartlet molds. Prick the base of each pastry case with a fork, then spoon in the soufflé mixture to two-thirds full.

Bake in a preheated oven at 400°F (200°C) for 20 minutes. Serve immediately.

MAKES 24

Pictured opposite: Classic Cheese Soufflé

CHEESE MOUSSE DUMPLINGS IN A SAFFRON SAUCE

QUENELLES DE FROMAGE SAUCE SAFFRAN

The word 'quenelle' comes from the Saxon word 'knyl', meaning 'to pound to a paste'. In these quenelles, the curd cheese takes the place of a pounded mixture of fish or meat, and the flavor and texture are the better for it.

QUENELLES
1 whole egg and 2 egg whites
1 lb. (500 g) curd cheese
sea salt and freshly ground black pepper
freshly grated nutmeg
juice and grated rind of 1/2 lemon
1 cup (2 oz., 60 g) soft whole-wheat
(wholemeal) breadcrumbs
12 large spinach leaves

SAUCE
1 oz. (30 g) butter
1 small onion, chopped
2/3 cup (5 fl. oz., 155 ml) dry vermouth
1 tablespoon tomato paste (purée)
1 avocado, pitted, skinned, and mashed
sea salt and freshly ground black pepper
pinch each of paprika and saffron
2/3 cup (5 fl. oz., 155 ml) heavy cream

Beat the egg, egg whites, and cheese together until smooth. Season with salt, pepper, and nutmeg, then add the lemon juice and rind. Blend in the breadcrumbs to form a smooth, thick paste.

Divide the paste into 12 pieces and mold into egg-shaped portions with two tablespoons. Place the quenelles on waxed paper on a baking sheet (tray) and put in the freezer for 10 minutes. Bake in an oven preheated at 375°F (190°C) for 15 minutes. Allow to cool.

Blanch the spinach leaves. Drain and spread out on a board. Wrap a leaf around each quenelle and place two quenelles on each serving plate.

For the sauce, heat the butter in a saucepan and sauté the onion until soft but not browned. Add the vermouth, tomato paste, and avocado. Season with salt, pepper, paprika, and saffron. Boil for 8 minutes. Stir the cream into the sauce and check the seasoning. Cook gently for a further 4 minutes.

Pour the sauce over the quenelles and garnish with a sprig of dill, a wedge of tomato and a slice of toasted brioche.

SERVES 6

GOAT'S CHEESE CUSHIONS WITH GREENGAGE SAUCE

LES FEUILLETÉS DE FROMAGE DE CHÈVRE AUX REINES CLAUDES

These light puff pastry parcels with a luscious filling are transformed into pure heaven by a simple sauce of the quintessentially French plum, the greengage.

CHEESE CUSHIONS
3/4 cup (6 oz., 185 g) fresh goat's cheese
1 clove garlic, crushed
1 tablespoon chopped fresh basil
1 tablespoon chopped pine kernels
sea salt and freshly ground black pepper
12 oz. (350 g) package of whole-wheat (wholemeal)
puff pastry *or* 1/2 quantity puff pastry (see p. 159)
egg, beaten, for glazing

SAUCE
12 oz. (375 g) ripe greengages, halved, skinned, and pitted
2 tablespoons redcurrant jelly
2 tablespoons Armagnac

TO SERVE
1/3 cup (3 fl. oz., 90 ml) heavy cream, warmed
fresh basil sprigs

Mash together the cheese, garlic, basil, and pine kernels. Taste (the goat's cheese may be salty) and season accordingly.

Roll out the pastry quite thinly. Cut out 12 circles about 3 in. (7.5 cm) in diameter. Use six of these circles to line six cupcake pans. Brush the edges of each with beaten egg.

Divide the cheese mixture between the pastry shells. Top with the remaining pastry circles and pinch the edges to seal well. Glaze with beaten egg.

Bake in a preheated oven at 400°F (200°C) for 15 to 20 minutes, until puffed and golden.

Meanwhile, make the sauce. Place the greengages, redcurrant jelly, and Armagnac in a blender or food processor and purée until smooth.

Spoon a little of the sauce onto six serving plates and serve a cheese cushion straight from the oven onto each plate. Make a little hole in the top of each cheese cushion and pour in a spoonful of cream. Garnish with the basil and serve at once with a side salad of bitter salad leaves.

SERVES 6

Pictured above right: Cream Cheese Custards with Lettuce and Watercress

CREAM CHEESE CUSTARDS WITH LETTUCE AND WATERCRESS

....

LES RAMEQUINS À LA POTAGÈRE

Cream cheese has a rich, yet bland, flavor. It makes a perfect base ingredient for a great many dishes, and can be enlivened by the addition of all manner of ingredients, from other cheeses to vegetables, herbs and spices. It is a very versatile ingredient which can be lightened with beaten egg whites and whipped cream or blended with creamed potato for a heavier mix. It lends itself to all kinds of uses: as a filling for pancakes, pastries and tarts, as a stuffing for mushrooms, other vegetables, and pastas, and as a sauce for a variety of dishes. In this dish it adds its creaminess to a delicately flavored custard.

8 oz. (250 g) cream cheese
5 eggs, beaten
1 teaspoon sea salt
freshly ground black pepper
freshly grated nutmeg

1¼ cups (10 fl. oz., 310 ml) milk
1 small bunch watercress, tough stalks discarded, cut into thin shreds
1 small soft-headed lettuce, leaves separated and cut into thin shreds
2 oz. (60 g) butter, softened
⅔ cup (5 fl. oz., 155 ml) light cream (optional)
3 tablespoons chopped fresh parsley, to garnish

In a bowl, beat the cream cheese and eggs to a soft, well-blended mixture. Season to taste with salt, pepper, and nutmeg.

Gradually stir in the milk. When you have a smooth, creamy mixture, add the shredded watercress and lettuce.

Liberally coat six ramekins with softened butter, then fill them to the brim with the mixture. Place in a water bath or bain marie. Bake in a preheated oven at 350°F (180°C) for 15 to 20 minutes.

Unmold the custards onto individual plates. Boil the cream quickly and pour over, or substitute a light vinaigrette. Sprinkle with parsley and serve.

SERVES 6

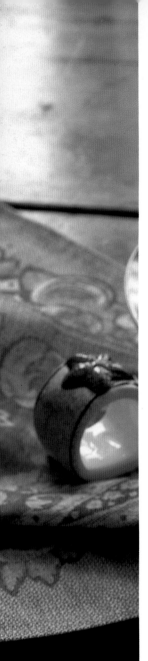

GOAT'S CHEESE FLAN

LE FROMAGE DU POITOU

Goats are sometimes called 'poor man's cows' — how derisive! Not only is goat's milk healthier than cow's milk, causing fewer allergic reactions, but gourmets almost always prefer goat's cheese to cow's milk varieties. The general name for any type of goat's milk cheese is 'chèvre', which covers a wide range of textures and strengths of flavor, from mild, soft, fresh cheeses to hard, well-aged, and strongly flavored ones. The Loire is well known for its goat's cheeses, but most regions of France have at least one variety. This recipe comes from Poitou, on the western coast of France.

PASTRY

2 cups (8 oz., 250 g) whole-wheat (wholemeal) flour
1/2 cup (4 oz., 125 g) butter
2 tablespoons Demerara (raw) sugar
1 egg, beaten

FILLING

8 oz. (250 g) goat's cheese, crust removed
1/4 cup (2 fl. oz., 60 ml) heavy cream
3/4 cup (3 oz., 90 g) whole-wheat (wholemeal) flour
3/4 cup (3 oz., 90 g) cornstarch (cornflour)
2 tablespoons orange liqueur
sea salt
5 eggs, separated
1/2 cup (4 oz., 125 g) diced angelica
2/3 cup (5 oz., 155 g) Demerara (raw) sugar,
finely ground

Prepare the pastry by rubbing the flour and butter to the consistency of fine breadcrumbs. Stir in the sugar and beaten egg to form a smooth dough. Roll into a ball and rest for 1 hour.

To make the filling, blend together the goat's cheese and cream. Gradually stir in the flour and cornstarch, then the orange liqueur, salt, beaten egg yolks, and, finally, the angelica. Make sure everything is thoroughly mixed.

In a separate bowl, beat the egg whites with a pinch of salt. When they hold firm peaks, start adding the sugar, a spoonful at a time, beating the egg whites back to firmness every time. Then fold the egg whites carefully into the cheese mixture.

Roll out the pastry and line a well-greased quiche pan. Pour in the cheese filling.

Bake in a preheated oven at 400°F (200°C) for 45 minutes to 1 hour, until golden.

Serve hot or cold with a light fruit salad.

SERVES 6

THREE-CHEESE PIE

TOURTE AUX TROIS FROMAGES

As well as cream cheese and Gruyère, this recipe uses Cantal, which is thought to be the oldest French cheese of all. Cantal is sometimes called French Cheddar, and just like the great British cheese, it has its commercially made variety, Laitier, which is made all year round in dairies (never huge factories, unlike some Cheddar), and its 'farmhouse' variety, Fermier, which is made during summer, and which you will rarely find outside the Auvergne region, where it is produced. It is covered by an 'appellation d'origine' — just like a good wine.

4 oz. (125 g) cream cheese
6 eggs, beaten
1 cup (4 oz., 125 g) diced Cantal cheese
1 cup (4 oz., 125 g) diced Gruyère cheese
1 cup (4 oz., 125 g) walnuts
1 small onion, chopped
1 tablespoon chopped fresh parsley
sea salt and freshly ground black pepper
1 1/2 quantities shortcrust pastry (see p. 158)

In a bowl, combine the cream cheese and eggs. Add the Cantal, Gruyère, walnuts, onion, and parsley and stir well, then season to taste with salt and pepper.

On a floured pastry board, roll out half the pastry in a circle 8 in. (20 cm) in diameter and about 1/4 in. (6 mm) thick. Line a greased 7-in. (17.5-cm) quiche pan.

Fill the pastry case with the cheese mixture; brush the edges of the pastry with water.

Roll out the other half of the pastry to the same thickness and diameter. Lay this over the filling, crimp the edges of the pastry together to seal, and trim with a sharp knife.

Bake in a preheated oven at 400°F (200°C) for 45 minutes to 1 hour.

Serve hot or cold with a green salad.

SERVES 8

Pictured opposite: Goat's Cheese Flan

BRIE FRITTERS

LES CROUSTILLANTS DE BRIE CHAMPENOIS

Talleyrand, the statesman and gourmet, dubbed Brie the King of Cheeses, and it was said by his critics that the only master he never betrayed was Brie!
There are many different types of Brie, but the main three are Brie de Meaux, Brie de Melun and Brie de Coulommiers. Brie de Meaux is made on farms. It is considered by many to be the 'true' Brie, and the one to which Talleyrand was so devoted. Brie de Melun is made in small dairies by traditional methods. It has a more pronounced flavor and smell than Brie de Meaux, and is slightly more salty and sharp. Brie de Coulommiers is usually factory-made and is enriched with cream to make it smooth and mild. It is in season from October to May, whereas the other two are best from October to June.

¹/₂ cup (2 oz., 60 g) whole-wheat (wholemeal) flour

2 eggs, beaten

¹/₂ cup (1 oz., 30 g) soft whole-wheat (wholemeal) breadcrumbs

¹/₂ cup (2 oz., 60 g) slivered, crushed almonds

1 x 1 lb. (500 g) piece of Brie, not too ripe, cut into eight triangles of roughly equal size

1¹/₄ cups (10 fl. oz., 310 ml) vegetable oil

Spread the flour on a plate. Pour the egg into another plate. Mix the breadcrumbs and almonds together in a third plate.

Coat each piece of Brie with flour, then with beaten egg, and lastly with the breadcrumb and almond mixture.

Heat the oil until just smoking and shallow-fry the fritters until golden-brown — this only takes a minute. Serve immediately.

VARIATION
Any soft cheese of this type can be prepared similarly: Camembert is the obvious one, but Pont l'Evêque, Caprice des Dieux, and many others, are just as good.

SERVES 4

Rich Cheesy Fritters

Les Beignets de Fromage à la Jurassienne

These delicious little fritters are a traditional dish of the beautiful Jura region, which produces Comté cheese.

Beignets

4 oz. (125 g) butter

1 cup (4 oz., 125 g) whole-wheat (wholemeal) flour

4 cups (1¾ imp. pints, 1 litre) milk

sea salt and freshly ground black pepper

freshly grated nutmeg

2 cups (8 oz., 250 g) grated Comté, Gruyère, *or* other hard cheese

4 egg yolks

Coating

½ cup (2 oz., 60 g) whole-wheat (wholemeal) flour

1 egg and 4 egg whites

3 cups (6 oz., 185 g) soft whole-wheat (wholemeal) breadcrumbs

½ cup (2 oz., 60 g) crushed, slivered almonds

2 large Golden Delicious apples, peeled, cored, and thickly sliced

vegetable oil, for shallow frying

Heat the butter in a large saucepan and stir in the flour to make a roux. Cook for a few minutes, without browning, stirring constantly.

Gradually whisk the milk into the roux, in four stages, making sure the mixture is smooth at the end of every stage. Season well with salt, pepper, and nutmeg, then stir in the cheese.

Beat the egg yolks lightly in a bowl and stir in 1¼ cups (10 fl. oz, 310 ml) sauce to make a thick paste. Return this to the pan of sauce, stirring well.

Pour into a deep, flat, earthenware dish measuring 8 x 4 in. (20 x 10 cm). Leave to cool and harden, refrigerating once it is cool enough.

When the paste is quite cold, turn it out onto a pastry board and cut into 2-in. (5-cm) squares.

Coat these *beignets* in the flour, then in the beaten egg and egg white mixture, then in the combined breadcrumbs and almonds. Repeat with the apple slices. Heat the oil in a deep skillet (frying pan) and sauté the *beignets* for ½ minute on each side. Drain and keep warm. Sauté the apple fritters for 2 minutes until golden-brown. Drain and serve both immediately.

SERVES 4

Brie Turnover

La Flamiche de Melun

Every region of France has its own variations of this type of cheese pastry. You could use shortcrust pastry to make this dish, but a puff pastry will produce a lighter yet richer dish.
To make your own celery salt, pound together in a mortar, or grind in a coffee mill, 1 teaspoon celery seeds to every ⅔ cup (4 oz., 125 g) sea salt.

Filling

2 oz. (60 g) butter, softened

3 oz. (90 g) ripe Brie de Melun

½ cup (2 oz., 60 g) whole-wheat (wholemeal) flour

1 egg, beaten

sea salt *or* celery salt

freshly ground black pepper

1 quantity puff pastry (see p. 159), chilled

1 egg, beaten, for glazing

Mix the butter and Brie together in a bowl until well combined. Add the flour and egg to form a very soft, fairly smooth paste. Season to taste with salt and pepper.

To assemble the dish, roll out the chilled pastry on a floured board to make a rectangle 10 x 5 in. (25 x 12.5 cm) and about ⅛ in. (3 mm) thick.

Cut the pastry into two squares. Place one square on a greased baking sheet (tray). Brush its edges with a little beaten egg.

Place the filling in the center of the square and cover it with the other square of pastry, crimping the edges with your fingers to seal well. Mark the top of the turnover with a criss-cross pattern and brush with the egg.

Bake in a preheated oven at 400°F (200°C) for 25 to 30 minutes.

Variations

A peeled and chopped apple can be added to the cheese filling for a more tangy flavor.

This filling can also be used in little quiches.

SERVES 4

Pictured opposite: Brie Fritters

HOT AND COLD DESSERTS

LES DESSERTS CHAUDS ET FROIDS

CREAM CHEESE MOUSSES WITH STRAWBERRY SAUCE

CRÉMETS AU COULIS DE FRAISE

Here is one of Normandy's best known desserts. If you can obtain true French 'fromage blanc' for this dish, so much the better. But cream cheese will certainly make a delicious dessert — albeit one much higher in calories!

1 cup (5 oz., 155 g) strawberries

2 tablespoons Demerara (raw) sugar

juice of ¼ lemon

2 oz. (60 g) cream cheese

¼ cup (2 fl. oz., 60 ml) heavy cream

extra 3 tablespoons Demerara (raw) sugar, ground to a powder

1 egg white

pinch of sea salt

strawberries, to garnish

Put the strawberries, sugar, and lemon juice in a blender or food processor and blend until a thick sauce forms. Chill this coulis for 20 minutes.

In a bowl, beat together the cream cheese and cream, then stir in 2 tablespoons of the extra powdered sugar.

In another bowl, whisk the egg white with a pinch of salt until stiff peaks form. Gradually whisk in the remaining 1 tablespoon of powdered sugar. Fold into the cream cheese.

Spoon the mixture into four molds that have drainage (either special heart-shaped molds with holes in the base, or you can punch holes in plastic yogurt containers and use these).

Place the molds in the refrigerator for 20 minutes (or the freezer for 10 minutes) to chill and drain. (Put a pan of some sort under the draining molds to catch the drips.)

To serve, spoon a little of the strawberry coulis onto four chilled plates, then unmold a cheese mousse over each. Decorate with tiny wild strawberries or slices of normal strawberries if none of the wild variety are available.

Serve at once.

Note: If you line any mold with clean muslin, it will prove much easier to unmold.

SERVES 4

RHUBARB SNOW WITH RASPBERRIES

NEIGE DE RHUBARBE AUX FRAMBOISES

Rhubarb is, in fact, a vegetable — in the past, its leaves were used like spinach — and yet it makes a whole host of delicious desserts. (Its leaves do, however, contain oxalic acid, which can be harmful.)
Rhubarb is a perfect base for a light dish such as this, its subtle flavor paired with aromatic fresh raspberries. I have chosen to use a liquid sweetener in this dish, making it good for diabetics and dieters alike, as well as for anyone who wants to finish a meal in style without feeling overly full.

1 lb. (500 g) rhubarb, trimmed and cut into chunks

1 tea bag

1 cup (5 oz., 155 g) raspberries, cleaned

½ cup (4 fl. oz., 125 ml) plain yogurt

½ cup (4 oz., 125 g) cottage cheese

12 drops liquid sweetener

2 egg whites

pinch of sea salt

Put the rhubarb in a saucepan of water, bring to the boil, and cook until tender. Remove from the heat and add the tea bag for 5 minutes, then discard. Leave to cool.

When cool, drain the rhubarb and place in a blender or food processor with half the raspberries. Blend to a purée.

Place in a bowl and beat in the yogurt and cottage cheese. Stir in the sweetener to taste.

In a separate bowl, beat the egg whites with the salt until stiff. Fold into the fruit mixture, then pour into tall glasses. Decorate with the remaining raspberries before serving.

SERVES 4

Pictured on previous pages: Cream Cheese Mousse with Strawberry Sauce
Pictured opposite: Rhubarb Snow with Raspberries

RASPBERRY CREAM WITH EAU DE VIE

VOLUPTÉ NUPTIALE AUX FRAMBOISES

The potent liqueurs of Alsace, called 'eau de vie', are flavored with various fruits, raspberry being one of my favorites. The raspberry is well suited to this 'water of life', since it is a fruit well known for its healing qualities. Raspberry leaf tea, with its astringent qualities, is good for sore throats, as a wash for wounds, and for settling stomach complaints. A spoonful of raspberry vinegar in a glass of warm water is a refreshing and stimulating drink, guaranteed to awaken even the sleepiest head in the morning!

5 oz. (155 g) silken tofu
1 tablespoon clear honey
4½ cups (1½ lb., 750 g) raspberries
2 tablespoons *framboise eau de vie* or other strawberry liqueur
3 egg whites
1 tablespoon superfine (caster) sugar
slices of papaya (pawpaw) and orange, to garnish
extra raspberries, to garnish

Put the tofu and honey in a blender or food processor and blend until smooth. Transfer this mixture to a bowl.

Purée the raspberries and liqueur, then pass through a strainer to remove the seeds. Stir the purée into the tofu mixture.

In a separate bowl, whisk the egg whites and sugar until stiff, then fold carefully into the fruit and tofu mixture.

Spoon into four tall cocktail-type glasses and decorate with the papaya, oranges, and extra raspberries. Serve at once.

SERVES 4

RASPBERRY AND HAZELNUT CASTLE

CHARTREUSE DE FRAMBOISE À LA CHANTILLY

Fresh raspberries are one of the real delights of summer. This rich dessert is for special occasions only.

½ cup (6 oz., 185 g) set (candied) honey
6 oz. (185 g) unsalted butter
1 cup (4 oz., 125 g) ground toasted hazelnuts
3 tablespoons raspberry liqueur
1 lb. (500 g) raspberries, cleaned
1¼ cups (10 fl. oz., 310 ml) heavy cream
4 drops vanilla extract (essence)
8 oz. (250 g) boudoir cookies (savoiardi biscuits)
extra raspberries, for garnish

Beat together the honey and butter until light and fluffy. Stir in the hazelnuts, then beat in the liqueur. Fold in the raspberries.

In a separate bowl, whisk together the cream and vanilla extract until quite stiff. Fold into the raspberry mixture.

Line the base of a round 6-in. (15-cm) soufflé dish or straight-sided cake pan with a circle of greased parchment or baking paper. Stand the biscuits up, sugar-side outward, around the side of the dish or pan. Spoon in the raspberry mixture and level the top.

Refrigerate for approximately 4 hours until chilled and set.

Turn the dessert out onto a chilled platter and peel off the paper. Decorate the top with the extra raspberries and serve at once.

SERVES 6

Pictured above right: Banana Mousse with Passion Fruit

BANANA MOUSSE WITH PASSION FRUIT

....

MOUSSELINE DE BANANE AUX
GRENADILLES

*Bananas and rum make a great combination, but it is a
heady mixture that needs to be offset with an aromatic
sharpness, such as that of the passion fruit. A sauce in
itself, a passion fruit simply needs to be halved and its
innards scooped out to produce a silky coating liquid,
dotted with tiny edible seeds.
These light mousses are second cousin to a jelly. They are
set, but creamy; smooth, but with the occasional bite
from chopped nuts and crystallized fruit.
What a perfect combination!*

4 ripe bananas, peeled and chopped

juice and grated rind of ¹/₂ lemon

2 tablespoons clear honey

2 tablespoons white rum

1¹/₄ cups (10 fl. oz, 310 ml) plain yogurt

3 tablespoons water

1 tablespoon agar-agar

2 eggs, separated

2 tablespoons chopped almonds

1 tablespoon chopped angelica

6 passion fruits

Put the bananas, lemon juice and rind, honey,
and rum in a blender or food processor and
blend until smooth. Turn out into a bowl and stir
in the yogurt.

Heat the water to boiling point, stir in the agar-
agar, and boil for 3 minutes. Beat into the banana
mixture, then beat in the egg yolks. Leave to cool
to the point of setting.

In a separate bowl, whisk the egg whites. Fold
into the mixture, lightly but thoroughly, along
with the almonds and angelica.

Spoon the mixture into 6 individual greased
ramekins or a single greased loaf pan. Chill until
set — about 4 hours.

Scoop the contents of the passion fruits out
onto 6 individual plates. Unmold a mousse onto
each plate and serve at once.

SERVES 6

GREENGAGE MOUSSE IN CHOCOLATE CUPS

MOUSSE DE REINE-CLAUDES AU CHOCOLAT

Sir William Gage of Suffolk brought the greengage (a sweet and white variety of plum) from the monastery of Chartreuse to my adopted land of England, and gave it his name. Thus, it seems appropriate, in a greengage dish, to use that very special liqueur made by the Carthusian monks of Chartreuse. Made with 130 herbs, its flavor is unique.

14 oz. (435 g) unsweetened (cooking) chocolate

2 teaspoons agar-agar

2 tablespoons water

1¼ cups (10 fl. oz., 310 ml) puréed stewed greengages

1¼ cups (10 fl. oz., 310 ml) plain yogurt

2 tablespoons yellow Chartreuse

Melt the chocolate and use to coat 16–20 paper muffin (patty-cake) cases (use three cases for each one to give sufficient thickness and strength). Allow to cool, then coat again. Chill.

In a saucepan, dissolve the agar-agar in the water. Bring to the boil and boil for 3 minutes before beating into the greengage purée. Then fold in the yogurt and liqueur.

Just as the mixture begins to set, spoon it into the chocolate cups. Allow to set before serving.

MAKES 16-20

Pictured opposite: Greengage Mousse in a Chocolate Cup

GREENGAGE PUDDING

LE CLAFOUTIS AUX REINE-CLAUDES

The most common version of this very traditional French dish is made with fresh black cherries. It certainly is delicious that way, but the more unusual fruit, the greengage, is worth sampling — and if you are in a hurry, it is far easier to stone greengages than cherries!

The French Reine-Claude greengage is the larger, sweeter, and possibly the best of all varieties of plum. Do try to seek it out for a real treat. If you cannot, this pudding, a specialty of the Limousin region of France, will bring out the best in even the more humble greengage varieties.

1 lb. (500 g) greengages, halved and pitted

⅔ cup (5 fl. oz., 155 ml) brandy

pinch of ground cinnamon

¾ cup (3 oz., 90 g) whole-wheat (wholemeal) flour

½ cup (4 oz., 125 g) Demerara (raw) sugar

4 eggs, beaten

pinch of sea salt

2 drops natural vanilla extract (essence)

¼ cup (2 fl. oz., 60 ml) vegetable oil

Put the greengages, brandy, and cinnamon in a bowl and leave to soak for 1 hour. Drain the plums and put any residual brandy to one side.

Preheat the oven to 400°F (200°C).

In another bowl, combine the flour, sugar, and eggs to make a smooth, thick batter. Stir in the salt and vanilla extract, then add the brandy.

Coat a shallow earthenware baking dish with the oil and heat it in the oven for 10 minutes. Remove from the oven. Pour in half the batter and bake on the top shelf of the oven for 15 to 20 minutes, until well-risen and puffy.

Remove the dish from the oven. Arrange the greengages on top of the batter and cover with the remaining batter. Bake for a further 40 minutes on the middle shelf, until golden and risen. Cooking the dish like this ensures that the bottom half of the batter is crisp and crusty, like a Yorkshire pudding, while the second layer is softer and more like a set custard.

Serve warm.

SERVES 6

RUSSIAN–FRENCH PEACH DESSERT

PASKAS DE COULIS DE PÊCHE DE MONTREUIL

The wonderful white peaches of Montreuil, where I spent some time before the war, still live in my memory. They are perfect for this French variation on a traditional Russian Easter dish.

3 oz. (90 g) softened butter

1/3 cup (3 oz., 90 g) Demerara (raw) sugar, ground to a powder

1 cup (3 oz., 90 g) ground almonds

2 tablespoons Kirsch *or* brandy

1 lb. (500 g) cream *or* curd cheese

4 large ripe peaches

juice of 1 lemon

6 drops orange blossom water

Beat together the butter and sugar until light and fluffy, then beat in the almonds and Kirsch or brandy. Fold in the cheese and stir until the mixture is smooth and creamy. Cover the bowl and place in the refrigerator for 1 hour.

Plunge the peaches into boiling water for a minute, then cut in half, remove the stones, and peel away the skins. Place in a bowl, toss with the lemon juice and orange water, and leave to marinate for a few minutes.

When ready to serve, spoon the cheese mixture into the upturned peach halves, rounding the tops neatly, and place two filled peach halves on each plate. Serve at once.

SERVES 4

Pictured opposite: Russian-French Peach Dessert

ROSÉ WINE AND WHITE PLUM JELLY

GELÉE DE VIN DE PROVENCE AUX MIRABELLES

This delicate sweet jelly uses agar-agar as a gelling agent. Agar, which is derived from seaweed, is as good as gelatin and does not rely on animal bones and hooves for its setting qualities.
Very little sugar is needed for this dish. The wine and the natural sugars of the fruit give the jelly most of the sweetness it needs.
Mirabelles are golden-white plums, about the size of a large olive, sweet to the taste and with very little acidity.

1 1/4 cups (10 fl. oz., 310 ml) *Rosé de Provence* wine or other rosé

1/3 cup (3 oz., 90 g) white sugar

2 teaspoons agar-agar

juice of 1 lemon

12 mirabelles, halved and pitted

12 sour cherries, pitted

1/3 cup (3 fl. oz., 90 ml) heavy cream, whipped

Bring the wine and sugar gently to the boil in a saucepan. Add the agar-agar and boil for 2 minutes. Stir in the lemon juice.

Remove from the heat and add the mirabelles, letting them soak in the hot liquid.

As the liquid cools, add the cherries.

Before the mixture sets, remove the fruit with a slotted spoon. Pour half the jelly into four tall glasses and allow to set. Spoon the fruit over this.

Reheat the remaining jelly just enough for it to become liquid again, then pour it over the fruit. Allow to set. The fruit should be suspended in jelly, halfway up the glasses.

Pipe rosettes of cream on the top of each glass, then serve.

SERVES 4

CANTALOUPE AND PEACH SHERBET

....

LE MELON GLACÉ NÉPAL

In the summer of 1937, I was working at the Hermitage Hotel, Le Touquet. One day, whilst taking a well-earned break on the sands, I saw an English nanny remonstrating with her little charge for hitting one of his French playmates on the head with a spade. Later, at a children's party at the hotel, I was to discover that the mischievous young aggressor was the future King of Nepal. Small children are alike in good and naughty behavior after all! We served this sherbet, and all the children were as good as gold. It is a cross between a water ice and the now-fashionable frozen yogurt.

1 medium cantaloupe (rockmelon), halved, skin removed, and seeds discarded
2 ripe peaches, skinned, halved, and pitted
1 tablespoon blanched almonds
1 cup (8 oz., 250 g) white sugar
2/3 cup (5 fl. oz., 155 ml) plain yogurt
2 egg whites
peach slices, to garnish (optional)
cantaloupe (rockmelon) balls, to garnish (optional)

Put the cantaloupe flesh, peaches, and blanched almonds in a blender or food processor and blend until smooth.

Spoon this purée into a shallow container, stir in the sugar and yogurt, and freeze until slushy.

In a bowl, beat the egg whites until stiff but not 'dry', then fold them into the semi-frozen sherbet. Return to the freezer to firm. Alternatively, use an ice-cream machine, following the relevant instructions for this procedure.

Remove the sherbet from the freezer just before serving to allow it to soften slightly. Spoon into tall-stemmed glasses and decorate with peach slices and cantaloupe balls, if desired.

SERVES 4

JELLIED STRAWBERRY CROWN

COURONNE DE FRAISES ROMANOFF

*Agar-agar is used to set this delicious piquant jelly.
The natural pectin in fresh apple juice helps, too.*

½ cup (4 fl. oz., 125 ml) fresh apple juice

2½ cups (1 imp. pint, 625 ml) fresh orange juice

¼ cup (2 fl. oz., 60 ml) fresh lemon juice

2 teaspoons agar-agar

3 cups (1 lb., 500 g) strawberries, cleaned and hulled

½ cup (6 oz., 185 g) honey

1 small cantaloupe (rockmelon), halved and
seeds discarded

¼ cup (2 fl. oz., 60 ml) Cointreau

Heat the apple, orange, and lemon juices together in a saucepan. When the liquid is almost boiling, sprinkle over the agar-agar, stir in to dissolve, and boil for 2 minutes.

Place the strawberries, honey, and half the thickened fruit juices in a blender or food processor and blend to a smooth purée, then stir in the remaining juices.

Rinse out an 8-in. (20-cm) crown dessert mold with cold water, then pour in the strawberry mixture. Place in the refrigerator to set and chill.

Meanwhile, use a melon baller to scoop out small balls of cantaloupe flesh. Place them in a bowl and pour the Cointreau over to marinate.

Turn out the strawberry crown onto a chilled serving plate and fill the center with the cantaloupe balls. Serve at once.

SERVES 6

Pictured left: Cantaloupe and Peach Sherbet

STRAWBERRY SOUFFLÉ

LE SOUFFLÉ AUX FRAISES

*This exquisite soufflé makes a light and flavorsome finish
to a rich dinner party. If you can, it is worth obtaining
'wild' or alpine strawberries to make this dish, as their
flavor and fragrance are much finer than that of
cultivated varieties. It is not difficult to grow your own,
and will certainly be worth the effort in terms of quality.*

2 oz. (60 g) butter

1½ cups (12 oz., 375 g) Demerara (raw) sugar

½ cup (4 fl. oz., 125 ml) water

3 cups (1 lb., 500 g) strawberries

1 tablespoon Grand Marnier

7 egg whites

Grease the insides of 8 individual ramekins with the butter, then use ¼ cup (2 oz., 60 g) sugar to lightly coat this butter lining.

In a saucepan, boil the water with the remaining 1¼ cups (8 oz., 250 g) sugar until a rich syrup is formed (which should read 260°F (125°C) on a sugar thermometer).

Meanwhile, having set aside 8 small, perfect strawberries for decoration, mash the remaining strawberries and pass through a strainer to remove the seeds. Put this purée in a saucepan and cook for 5 minutes to reduce the moisture.

When the sugar syrup has become very sticky and a drop put in cold water is hard and brittle, add it to the strawberry purée. Cook for 3 minutes more, stir in the liqueur, then set aside to cool.

In a very clean bowl, beat the egg whites until they hold firm peaks. Add the last ¼ cup (2 oz., 60 g) sugar, a teaspoon at a time, beating the egg whites back to firmness between each addition.

Stir half the strawberry purée into the egg whites, cutting with a criss-cross motion until well mixed. Then fold the rest in lightly.

Fill the ramekins to the brim with the soufflé mixture. Level the tops and run the back of a teaspoon around the rim of each ramekin to make a channel between it and the mixture. This ensures that the top rises evenly, making a more attractive finished dish.

Place on a baking sheet (tray) in the center of a preheated oven and bake at 400°F (200°C) for 15 to 20 minutes, until the soufflés are well risen.

Decorate each soufflé with a fresh strawberry and serve at once.

SERVES 8

NECTARINE AND CHABLIS ICE

LE SORBET AUX BRUGNONS

Here, nectarines are puréed in a delicate sorbet with good French wine and natural yogurt. I have chosen to use Chablis, which is perfect for a special occasion — dry, yet mellow enough to give a full flavor to the dish. However, any dry white wine with a suitable depth will suffice, and you can save your 'premiér crû' to drink with the meal.

4 large, ripe nectarines, pitted and cut into pieces
2 cups (16 fl. oz., 500 ml) water
²/3 cup (5 fl. oz., 155 ml) Chablis
1 cup (8 oz., 250 g) white sugar
²/3 cup (5 fl. oz., 155 ml) plain yogurt
2 egg whites

TO SERVE
½ cup (4 fl. oz., 125 ml) light whipping cream
Cointreau
orange peel, to garnish

Put the nectarine flesh in a saucepan with the water and cook until tender. Purée in a blender or food processor until smooth.

Return the purée to the saucepan. Add the Chablis and sugar, and cook, stirring, until the sugar is dissolved. Boil for 2 to 3 minutes.

Cool slightly before stirring in the yogurt, then pour into a freezer tray. Freeze until slushy.

In a bowl, whisk the egg whites until stiff but not 'dry'. Fold lightly into the semi-frozen sorbet. Return to the freezer and freeze until firm. Alternatively, use an ice-cream machine, following the relevant instructions for this procedure.

Flavor the cream with a dash of Cointreau, then pour a pool of cream onto each serving dish. Top with scoops of sorbet and garnish with fine strips of orange peel.

SERVES 4

FRUIT COMPOTE

LA COMPOTE DU MENDIANT

This delicious dessert is often cooked in the French countryside and varies in composition between regions. Tea is perfect for soaking the dried fruit, although you will often find that wine is used, especially the local 'vin ordinaire' in the wine-producing regions. In northern France you will even find the dried fruits soaked in beer! To make a more nourishing dessert, add the juice of an orange to the soaking liquid, as dried fruit loses its vitamin C. The 'mendiant' of the name comes from the mendicant friars, whose somber habit the rich, dark fruits of this dish are said to resemble.

3³/4 cups (1¹/2 imp. pints, 875 ml) freshly brewed tea of your choice
2 of each of the following dried fruits: apples, peaches, apricots, and prunes
¹/2 cup (3 oz., 90 g) seedless raisins
1 stick cinnamon
¹/4 cup (2 oz., 60 g) Demerara (raw) sugar
¹/2 cup (6 oz., 185 g) clear honey
grated rind and juice of 1 lemon
grated rind and juice of 1 orange
¹/2 cup (3 oz., 90 g) blanched almonds

Brew the tea for 5 minutes, then pour it over the dried fruit, which has been combined in a bowl, and leave to soak overnight.

Next day, put the fruits with the tea in a saucepan. Add the cinnamon, sugar, honey, and the lemon and orange rind and cook very gently for 15 to 20 minutes, then allow to cool.

Before serving, stir in the lemon and orange juice and the almonds. Serve in individual bowls as a dessert or as a refreshing breakfast dish. Frangipane cream (see p. 137) makes a good dessert accompaniment to this compote.

SERVES 6

Pictured opposite: Nectarine and Chablis Ice, and Fruit Compote

PEAR AND NUT TART

GALETTE DE POIRES AUX NOIX

*Dessert pears, such as William, Doyenne du Comice,
and Bon Chretien, are best for modern tastes because,
when ripe, they are sweet and juicy and little extra sugar
(if any) is needed during cooking. This dessert combines
pears with a delicate and delicious pastry speckled with
the greens and golds of ground pistachio nuts.*

PASTRY
2 cups (8 oz., 250 g) all-purpose (plain) flour
1/2 cup (2 oz., 60 g) ground pistachio nuts
1 tablespoon confectioner's (icing) sugar
pinch of sea salt
5 oz. (155 g) butter
1 egg yolk

PASTRY CREAM
1/4 cup (2 oz., 60 g) superfine (caster) sugar
1 egg plus 1 egg yolk
1 tablespoon all-purpose (plain) flour
1 heaped tablespoon cornstarch (cornflour)
1 1/4 cup (10 fl. oz., 310 ml) milk
few drops vanilla extract (essence) *or* 1 tablespoon
Poire William liqueur *or* Kirsch

TOPPING
3 ripe pears, peeled, halved, and cored
juice of 1 lemon

4 tablespoons apricot jam
2 tablespoons toasted, slivered almonds

For the pastry, mix together the flour, nuts,
sugar, and salt in a bowl. Rub in the butter,
then stir in the egg yolk to form a smooth pastry
dough. Wrap in plastic wrap and chill for 1 hour.

Meanwhile, prepare the pastry cream. Beat
together the sugar, egg and egg yolk, then beat in
the flour and cornstarch. Add a little of the milk, if
needed, to form a smooth paste.

Heat the remaining milk in a saucepan until
hot. Beat into the paste, then return the entire
mixture to the pan. Stir over a low heat until
thickened and smooth. Set aside to cool.

Roll out the chilled dough and line a 9-in. (23-
cm) loose-bottomed flan pan with it. Line the
dough with parchment or baking paper and baking
beans and bake blind at 190°F (375°C) for 10
minutes. Remove the paper and beans and return
to the oven to bake for a further 12 to 15 minutes.
Allow to cool.

Beat the vanilla extract or liqueur into the
cooled pastry cream, then spread this evenly over
the base of the tart shell.

Toss the pears in about half the lemon juice.
Drain well and arrange attractively on the pastry
cream, radiating out from the center of the tart.

Melt the jam with a tablespoonful or so of the
lemon juice. Brush over the tart and sprinkle with
almonds. Allow the jam to cool and set. Serve cool
but not chilled.

SERVES 4

PEAR AND CHOCOLATE CREAMS

....

LES POIRES AU CHOCOLAT SAINT-LOUIS

*Pears form the heart of many classic French desserts —
poached in red wine as Poires Belle-Angevine,
Vigneronne or Richelieu, poached in port for Poires Alma
and, perhaps most famous of all (and most popular with
children), served with ice-cream and hot chocolate sauce
as Poires Belle-Hélène.*

*This dish has echoes of a number of dishes, and the best
qualities of all, with brioche as its base and
chocolate–rum custard covering the pears, which poach
in their own juices as the custard bakes.*

2 small brioches, cut into 6 rounds

2 ripe pears*, peeled, cored, and diced

2¹/₂ cups (1 imp. pint, 625 ml) creamy milk

4 oz. (125 g) unsweetened (cooking) chocolate

3 eggs, beaten

2 tablespoons rum

white sugar (optional)

Fit the 6 brioche rounds neatly into the bases of
seaparate greased ramekins. Distribute the
diced pear between these 6 ramekins.

In a saucepan, heat the milk and melt the
chocolate in it. Allow to cool before beating in the
eggs and rum — a little sugar may also be added if
you wish.

Pour this chocolate custard into the molds.
Place in a water bath or bain marie so that the
water comes halfway up the ramekins. Bake in the
center of a preheated oven at 400°F (200°C) for
25 minutes.

Serve hot in their dishes, or allow to cool so
that the little custards can be turned out.

* Laurousse Agricole, Doyenne d'Hiver, Doyenne
du Comice, and Beurre Bachelier are suggested.

SERVES 6

BLACKCURRANT BRULÉE

....

CRÈME BRULÉE AU CASSIS

*Despite its French name, this dish stems from an
invention of Trinity College, Cambridge, some 300
years ago. Nowadays, in looking to reduce the richness
of our desserts, a brulée is often married with sharp
fruits, as here, and yogurt is substituted for part or
all of the original cream.*

*Choose a fruit yogurt of very high quality for this dish
(not one of those synthetic, highly colored concoctions so
often found on supermarket shelves). If you cannot find
anything of superior quality, use plain Greek yogurt.*

10 oz. (310 g) fresh or frozen blackcurrants

8 tablespoons water

2 level teaspoons cornstarch (cornflour)

a little white sugar, to taste

1¹/₄ cups (10 fl. oz., 310 ml) blackcurrant yogurt

4 heaped teaspoons Demerara (raw) sugar

¹/₄ cup (1 oz., 30 g) slivered almonds

Put the blackcurrants and water in a saucepan.
Cover with a lid and cook gently until soft.
Spoon out a little of the liquid and beat with the
cornflour to make a smooth paste, then stir this
back into the saucepan.

Bring the berries to the boil and simmer for 1 to
2 minutes to thicken. Taste and sweeten with sugar
if necessary. Set aside to cool.

When cool, spoon the mixture into 4 ramekins,
then spread with enough of the yogurt to
completely cover the blackcurrants.

Sprinkle sugar and almonds over. Place under a
very hot broiler (griller) to caramelize the sugar
and toast the almonds.

Chill until the sugar topping has set, then serve.

SERVES 4

Pictured above left: Pear and Nut Tart

APPLE FLAN, NORMANDY-STYLE

BOURDIN NORMANDE

This rich dessert, with its use of cream, apples, and Calvados, could only come from Normandy, with its lush pastures and bountiful orchards.

PASTRY

1¾ cups (6 oz., 185 g) whole-wheat (wholemeal) flour

2 cups (8 oz., 250 g) unbleached all-purpose (plain) flour

pinch of sea salt

1 teaspoon mixed spice

1 teaspoon Demerara (raw) sugar, ground to a powder

¼ cup (1 oz., 30 g) toasted almonds, finely crushed

4 oz. (125 g) butter

½ cup (4 fl. oz., 125 ml) water

FILLING

1½ lbs. (750 g) dessert apples, peeled, cored, and thinly sliced

⅓ cup (4 oz., 125 g) honey

2 eggs, beaten

¼ cup (2 fl. oz., 60 ml) heavy cream

¼ cup (2 oz., 60 g) Demerara (raw) sugar

1 tablespoon Calvados

1 tablespoon toasted, slivered almonds

Sift the two flours, salt, spice, and sugar into a bowl, adding back any bran left in the sieve. Stir the almonds into the mixture.

Rub the butter in to form a breadcrumb-like mixture. Add water a little at a time to make a smooth dough. Roll the pastry into a ball, place in plastic wrap, and refrigerate for 1 hour.

Roll the chilled dough out thinly. Grease an 8-in. (20-cm) flan pan and line with the pastry, pressing it in firmly. Trim the edges.

Layer the apples around the pastry shell. Drizzle over the honey. Cook in a preheated oven at 425°F (220°C) for 30 minutes.

Meanwhile, beat together the eggs, cream, sugar, and Calvados in a bowl.

When the apples are softened and turning golden, pour this mixture over them and return to the oven for a further 20 minutes. The custard should be golden and set.

Remove from the oven, sprinkle with almonds, and serve hot or cold.

VARIATIONS

Use yogurt instead of cream for a lighter dish.

For a truly spectacular finish to your meal, flame the tart with warmed Calvados just before serving!

SERVES 6

APPLE AND BLACKCURRANT MOUSSE

MOUSSELINE DE POMMES AU CASSIS

Apples lend themselves well to being combined with a great many fruits, but I think you will find that this blend of sharp cooking apples and tangy blackcurrants is quite unbeatable. You could use eating apples if you prefer a mellower taste, but the cream and eggs do add a certain mildness to the dish, which I find is nicely offset by the slight sharpness of the fruits. This is a very refreshing finish to a meal.

1½ lbs. (750 g) cooking apples, peeled, cored, and sliced

2 oz. (60 g) butter

2 cups (8 oz., 250 g) Demerara (raw) sugar

2 cups (8 oz., 250 g) blackcurrants, stems discarded, washed, and drained

4 eggs, separated

1 cup (2 oz., 60 g) whole-wheat (wholemeal) sponge cake crumbs

2 teaspoons arrowroot

¼ cup (2 fl. oz., 60 ml) water

½ cup (4 fl. oz., 125 ml) heavy cream, whipped

extra blackcurrants, to garnish

Put the apple, butter and three-quarters of the sugar in a saucepan. Cook very gently until the apple is soft and mushy, about 15 minutes, then pass the apples through a strainer and return the purée to the saucepan.

Stir the blackcurrants into the apple purée. If preferred, purée the blackcurrants in a blender or food processor before stirring into the apples.

Mix the egg yolks and cake crumbs together, then stir into the fruit mixture.

Combine the arrowroot and water, then stir into the fruit. Reheat until the mixture bubbles and thickens. Cook for a minute to completely cook the starch, but no longer.

In a separate bowl, beat the egg whites until stiff, then stir in the remaining sugar and beat again. Fold this egg white and sugar mixture into the hot fruit and mix well. Pour into fluted glasses and chill in the refrigerator.

Serve topped with whipped cream and a few extra blackcurrants.

SERVES 6

Pictured opposite: Apple Flan, Normandy-style

LAYERED CHERRY CHEESECAKE WITH LIQUEUR

LE MONTMORENCY AU FROMAGE

Cherries are grown all over France but the best come from the Burgundy region and Montmorency in the Ile-de-France. The best variety for this dish is the 'griotte', or red Morello cherry, which is more sour than an ordinary eating cherry and adds an appealing piquancy. This recipe may look rather involved but each stage is very simple to execute, and once prepared and assembled, the dish makes a spectacular finish to a special dinner.

1 cup (6 oz., 185 g) pitted sour red cherries
1/4 cup (2 fl. oz., 60 ml) mixed Kirsch and cherry brandy

FILLING
3 oz. (90 g) cream cheese
1/4 cup (2 fl. oz., 60 ml) heavy cream, whipped
1 tablespoon whole-wheat (wholemeal) flour
2 egg whites
pinch of sea salt
1/4 cup (2 oz., 60 g) Demerara (raw) sugar

1 quantity sweet shortcrust pastry (see p. 158)
2 tablespoons cherry jelly (jam)
1/2 wholemeal sponge that has been sliced horizontally

Soak the cherries in the liqueurs for at least 10 minutes. Meanwhile, prepare the filling. Blend the cream cheese, cream, and flour together in a bowl until well combined.

In a separate bowl, beat the egg whites with the salt until stiff. Add the sugar and beat until stiff again. Fold into the cream cheese mixture.

Roll out the chilled pastry to a thickness of 1/8 in. (3 mm) and line a well-greased, 9-in. (23-cm) cheesecake pan with it. Trim the edges. Spread with the jelly.

Lay the sponge on top of the jelly-coated base, cut side upwards. Arrange the cherries over the sponge and sprinkle with any remaining liqueur.

Pour the filling evenly over the cherries and bake in a preheated oven at 375°F (190°C) for 30 to 35 minutes until golden-brown. Halfway through cooking, remove the cheesecake from the oven and run a knife around the edge of the filling to prevent a skin from forming, which would cause it to balloon up rather than rise evenly.

Allow to cool before serving.

SERVES 6-8

CHERRY BREAD PUDDING

PAIN DE CERISES DE COMPIÈGNE

In this fruit-bread dessert, the bread is reduced to rich, fruit-speckled crumbs before being amalgamated with fat, ripe cherries, suspended in an eggy custard, and soaked in cherry brandy — so simple a way to use up stale bread, yet so special!

3 cups (24 fl. oz., 750 ml) milk
1/3 cup (3 oz., 90 g) Demerara (raw) sugar
1 cup (2 oz., 60 g) stale fruit-loaf breadcrumbs
5 eggs, separated
6 oz. (185 g) butter
1 1/2 lb. (750 g) pitted black cherries
pinch of sea salt
2 teaspoons superfine (caster) sugar
1/4 cup (1 oz., 30 g) chopped nuts
1/4 cup (2 fl. oz., 60 ml) cherry brandy
light whipping cream, to serve

Bring the milk and sugar to a boil, then remove from the heat.

Place the breadcrumbs in a bowl and pour the milk over. Mix well and set aside to cool a little.

Beat the egg yolks and butter into the crumb mixture, then stir in the cherries.

In a separate bowl, whisk the egg whites with the salt and sugar, then fold lightly into the custard mixture.

Grease an ovenproof dish 2 in. (5 cm) deep and 8 in. (20 cm) in diameter. Pour the mixture into the dish and sprinkle with the nuts.

Bake in a preheated oven at 400°F (200°C) for 35 minutes. Cool. Sprinkle with cherry brandy. Set aside to absorb the brandy before unmolding.

Serve with cream.

SERVES 6

Pictured right: Baked Rum and Raisin Batter Pudding

BAKED RUM AND RAISIN BATTER PUDDING

LE FAR BRETON

Breton cooking is abundant with inexpensive sweet dishes, which are quick and easy to make and extremely nourishing — the crêpe being an obvious example. The 'far' is a less well known but no less enjoyable example of the cuisine of Brittany. It can be varied endlessly, from a very basic mixture with plain raisins to a more luxurious dish with plums, apricots, cherries, or apples, soaked in an appropriate liqueur. For this recipe, I have stayed with the traditional raisin filling, but have given it a bit of luxury by soaking the raisins in rum first. Compare this dish with the Greengage Pudding (see p. 118). They are similar in their basic ingredients yet quite unique when cooked. Try both and decide which you like best — most likely you will enjoy both equally.

1 cup (5 oz., 155 g) seedless raisins
2/3 cup (5 fl. oz., 155 ml) rum
2 cups (8 oz., 250 g) whole-wheat (wholemeal) flour
large pinch of sea salt
6 eggs, beaten
5 cups (2 imp. pints, 1.25 litres) milk
1/2 cup (4 oz., 125 g) Demerara (raw) sugar,
ground to a powder
2 oz. (60 g) butter

Soak the raisins in the rum for several hours. Then put the flour and salt into a large bowl. Stir in the beaten eggs and mix well.

Heat a quarter of the milk to boiling point, then add gradually to the flour and egg, whisking to make a smooth batter.

Stir in the remaining milk, sugar, and raisins with any rum left from the soaking.

Grease a shallow, round earthenware baking dish, 8 in. (20 cm) in diameter, and pour in the batter. Bake for 1 hour 15 minutes in a preheated oven at 375°F (190°C).

Serve cold, cut into slices.

SERVES 6

CARAMELIZED UPSIDE-DOWN APPLE TART

LA TARTE TATIN

This delicious dessert was created by two elderly Frenchwomen who ran a very successful restaurant in Paris. It is a classic in France, yet very few chefs in other parts of the world have featured it. I hope this situation will soon be remedied, because it is a very good, and rather special, dessert.
Of all the varieties of apple, the most suited to sweet dishes of this sort are the Cox's Orange Pippin and the French Golden Delicious. Apples are rich in pectin so, once poached, they will help set a cold mousse or a purée of apples and berries.

¾ cup (6 oz., 185 g) Demerara (raw) sugar

2 tablespoons (1 oz., 30 g) butter

¼ cup (2 fl. oz., 60 ml) water

1 lb. (500 g) apples, peeled, cored, and halved

1 quantity sweet shortcrust pastry (see p. 158)

Cook the sugar, butter, and water together in a saucepan to make a caramel.

Pour into an ovenproof glass flan dish, spreading the caramel out to cover the entire dish.

Arrange the apple halves over the caramel.

Roll out the pastry, which should be about ¼ in. (6 mm) thick, to fit the flan dish and lay this over the apple halves.

Bake in a preheated oven at 400°F (200°C) for 35 to 40 minutes. Remove from the oven and allow to stand for 6 minutes.

Run a knife round the dish to loosen the tart, then turn out upside-down onto a flat serving dish.

SERVES 6-8

PRUNE AND APPLE ROLL WITH ARMAGNAC

ROULADE DE PRUNEAUX D'AGEN

In this roulade, prunes are matched with the sharpness of apples, the bite of walnuts, and the warmth of spices.

DOUGH

1 heaped tablespoon (⅔ oz., 20 g) compressed fresh yeast

⅓ cup (5 fl. oz., 155 ml) mixed milk and water

2 tablespoons honey

2 cups (8 oz., 250 g) whole-wheat (wholemeal) flour

pinch of sea salt

¼ cup (1 oz., 30 g) cornstarch (cornflour)

2 oz. (60 g) butter

FILLING

1 cup (4 oz., 125 g) chopped prunes, soaked in tea *or* in fruit juice with a dash of liqueur

1 cup (4 oz., 125 g) thinly sliced apples

1 cup (4 oz., 125 g) chopped walnuts

⅓ cup (3 oz., 90 g) Demerara (raw) sugar

1 teaspoon mixed spice

2 tablespoons Armagnac *or* Calvados

beaten egg, to glaze

sour cream, to serve

In a bowl, cream together the yeast, milk and water, and honey. Leave in a warm place to ferment for 10 minutes.

Place the flour, cornstarch, and salt in a bowl, and place this in an oven, preheated at 400°F (200°C), for 4 minutes to warm.

Make a well in the warmed flour and pour in the yeast mixture. Knead well to form a ball of elastic dough. Cover the bowl with a cloth and leave to rise for 30 minutes.

Knock back the dough, knead in the butter and roll the dough into a rectangle ¼ in. (5 mm) thick. Lay the prunes and apple over the dough, then sprinkle with nuts, sugar, spices, and liqueur. Roll the dough up from the longer side and pinch the edges to seal in the filling. Place on a greased baking sheet (tray), seam side down. Cover with a dampened cloth and leave to rise for 30 minutes.

Glaze the roll with beaten egg and bake on the middle shelf in the preheated oven for 35 to 40 minutes, until golden. Allow to cool before slicing into rounds. Serve with sour cream.

SERVES 8

Pictured opposite: Caramelized Upside-down Apple Tart

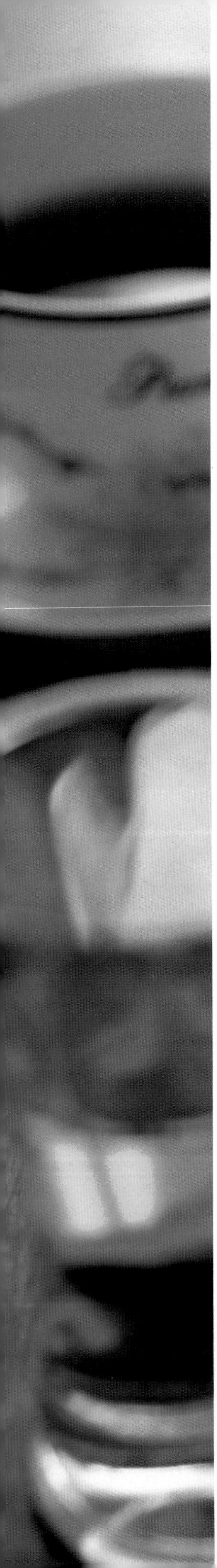

CHOCOLATE–LIQUEUR CREAM

MARQUISE AU CHOCOLAT

Variations on this dish are to be found in all the best restaurants in Paris or, indeed, in good French restaurants all over the world. It is always a favorite, since there are few people who do not find the combination of chocolate, cream, and liqueur irresistible. I have been serving the Marquise to my customers all my working life, and this particular recipe, using Grand Marnier and brandy to flavor the chocolate cream, has probably been the most popular.
It is a very rich dessert, so do not be tempted to serve your guests too much. This recipe will fill four ⅔-cup (5-fl. oz., 155-ml) ramekins, but if it is being served at the end of a rich or several-course dinner, it could easily stretch to six servings in smaller dishes without anyone feeling in the least deprived.

4 oz. (125 g) unsweetened (cooking) chocolate, broken up

4 eggs, separated

¼ cup (2 fl. oz., 60 ml) Grand Marnier

¼ cup (2 fl. oz., 60 ml) brandy

½ cup (4 fl. oz., 125 ml) heavy cream, whipped

pinch of sea salt

Put the chocolate in a bowl over a saucepan of hot water until it melts.

Put the egg yolks into another bowl and pour the melted chocolate over them. Stir to blend well.

Add the Grand Marnier, brandy, and cream. Mix all these ingredients together thoroughly.

In a separate bowl, beat the egg whites with the salt. Fold this mixture carefully into the chocolate cream so that it is completely combined but still light and fluffy.

Spoon into individual ramekins and refrigerate for 2 hours before serving.

VARIATIONS

This cream is delicious served with a compote of pears. It can also be heated and used as a sauce for profiteroles, ice-cream, or *Poires Belle-Hélène*. It can be mixed with an equal amount of chestnut paste to make a delicious *Mont Blanc* or to use as a filling for a gâteau. Other liqueurs can be substituted for the Grand Marnier — Tia Maria will add a pleasant coffee flavor, for example.

SERVES 4–6

CHESTNUT AND CHOCOLATE GÂTEAU

GÂTEAU DE GRASSE AUX MARRONS GLACÉS

This rich, chilled 'cake' from Provence needs no cooking. It will keep for up to a week in the refrigerator.

7 oz. (225 g) unsalted butter

½ cup (6 oz., 185 g) set (candied) honey

2 cups (1½ lbs., 750 g) unsweetened chestnut paste (purée)

14 oz. (435 g) unsweetened (cooking) chocolate, broken up

6 *marrons glacés* (crystallized chestnuts)

1 tablespoon confectioner's (icing) sugar (optional)

Beat together the butter and honey until well mixed. Then add the chestnut paste and beat again until smooth.

Place half the chocolate in a bowl over a saucepan of hot water to melt. Stir into the chestnut mixture and blend well.

Carefully line an 8-in. (20-cm) cake pan with waxed (greaseproof) paper. Pour the mixture into this, then place in the refrigerator to set and chill.

Meanwhile, melt the remaining chocolate until liquid, then pour onto a clean marble or plastic surface. When set, scrape with a palette knife to form curled shavings.

When the cake is set and chilled, turn out onto a serving platter and peel away the paper. Decorate with the *marrons glacés*, the chocolate shavings, and, if wished, a dusting of sugar. Serve cut into wedges like a baked cake.

SERVES 6

Pictured opposite: Chocolate-Liqueur Cream

CHESTNUT AND CHOCOLATE ROLL WITH PISTACHIO CREAM SAUCE

LA ROULADE DE MARRONS CHOCOLATÉS

Try to get some marrons glacés (chestnuts cooked in a rich syrup until crystallized — and France's greatest confectionery invention) to decorate this dessert.

CHESTNUT AND CHOCOLATE ROLL
2 lbs. (1 kg) chestnut paste (purée)
2 tablespoons dark rum *or* noisette liqueur
¼ cup (2 oz., 60 g) Demerara (raw) sugar, ground to a powder
8 oz. (250 g) unsweetened (cooking) chocolate
⅔ cup (5 fl. oz., 155 ml) heavy cream

PISTACHIO CREAM SAUCE
3 egg yolks
⅓ cup (3 oz., 90 g) Demerara (raw) sugar, ground to a powder
1¼ cups (10 fl. oz., 310 ml) milk
1 teaspoon arrowroot
4 tablespoons water
¾ cup (3 oz., 90 g) shelled and skinned pistachio nuts, chopped
2 tablespoons dark rum *or* noisette liqueur

Mash the chestnut purée and stir in half the liqueur. Mix well. Test for sweetness. Add the sugar to your taste and mix well again.

Melt the chocolate in a bowl over a saucepan of hot water. Remove from the heat and blend in the cream. Allow to cool and thicken slightly.

Spread the chestnut purée into a rectangle about 10 x 4 in. (25 x 10 cm) on a sheet of very clean plastic wrap. Spread the chocolate paste evenly over the chestnut paste, then lift one end of the plastic wrap and carefully roll the rectangle up as you would for a jelly roll (Swiss roll). Place in the refrigerator to chill for 20 minutes.

Meanwhile, make the pistachio cream. Beat the egg yolks and sugar together in a bowl. Boil the milk and pour it in slowly, stirring constantly.

Blend the arrowroot and water together. Stir this into the egg and milk mixture along with the pistachio nuts, then return to the saucepan and heat for 6 minutes to thicken and cook the sauce. Flavor with the reserved liqueur.

Cut the roll into slices and serve with the pistachio cream sauce.

SERVES 8

SUMMER SABAYON

LES FRUITS ROUGES AU FOUR

Here the rich, ripe fruits of summer are dressed in a foamy and frothy sauce — perfect for finishing any meal in light and simple style.

1½ cups (8 oz., 250 g) raspberries, cleaned
1½ cups (8 oz., 250 g) strawberries, cleaned and hulled
1½ cups (12 oz., 375 g) black cherries, pitted
2 tablespoons Grand Marnier
3 egg yolks
⅓ cup (3 oz., 90 g) Demerara (raw) sugar, ground to a powder
⅔ cup (5 fl. oz., 155 ml) sour cream

Put the raspberries, strawberries, and cherries in a bowl with the Grand Marnier and set aside to marinate.

In a bowl, whisk the egg yolks and sugar together. Place the bowl over a pan of just-simmering water and continue whisking until the mixture increases in volume and thickens. This will take about 6 minutes.

Gradually whisk in the sour cream and continue to whisk until the mixture is like a fluffy custard. This will take about 4 minutes.

Set aside a few pieces of fruit for decoration. Place the remaining fruit and the liqueur in individual shallow glass bowls.

Cover with custard and place under a hot broiler (griller) to brown slightly.

Decorate each bowl with the reserved fruit and serve at once.

SERVES 8

Baked Rice Mold with Apricots and Frangipane Cream

Les Abricots à la Bourdaloue

The best apricots are cultivated in the south of France, in Roussilon, Provence, and the Vallée du Rhone. They are among the fruits most commonly used in confectionery, baking, and jams in France, as anyone who has sampled a breakfast of coffee, croissants, and the ubiquitous apricot jam in a French hotel will confirm! This is a rich and filling dessert, but it is also one of the most nutritionally complete sweet dishes you can eat. Many of you will recognize instantly that the rice mold is made along the same lines as a traditional rice pudding. But rice-pudding haters should not let this put them off because this dish bears no resemblance to the stodgy, bland, and sickly 'nursery' pudding of childhood.

RICE MOLD

2½ cups (1 imp. pint, 625 ml) water

1 cup (7 oz., 225 g) short-grain brown rice

5 cups (2 imp. pints, 1.25 litres) milk

½ cup (4 oz., 125 g) Demerara (raw) sugar

4 oz. (125 g) butter

pinch of sea salt

1 vanilla pod *or* 3 drops natural vanilla extract (essence)

6 egg yolks

FRANGIPANE CREAM

2½ cups (1 imp. pint, 625 ml) milk

½ cup (4 oz., 125 g) Demerara (raw) sugar

½ cup (2 oz., 60 g) cornstarch (cornflour)

1 egg

3 egg yolks

1 cup (4 oz., 125 g) ground almonds

2 drops natural almond (extract) essence *or* 4 tablespoons anisette liqueur

APRICOTS

18 firm, ripe apricots, washed and wiped

1¼ cups (10 fl. oz., 310 ml) water

½ cup (4 oz., 125 g) Demerara (raw) sugar

2 tablespoons Kirsch

To prepare the rice mold, bring the water to the boil, add the rice, and cook for 8 minutes. Drain the rice and discard the water.

Bring the milk and sugar to the boil. Add the rice, half the butter, salt, and vanilla pod (if using vanilla extract, do not add yet). Cover the saucepan with a lid and lower the heat. Cook for 30 to 35 minutes until the rice is well cooked and almost dry. It will have a pastry-like consistency instead of falling apart into individual grains.

Remove from the heat and mix in the egg yolks well. If using vanilla extract, add it now.

Grease a 2½-quart (4-imp. pint, 2.5-litre) dessert mold with the remaining butter and fill with the rice mixture. Place in a water bath or bain marie half-filled with water and bake in a preheated oven at 400°F (200°C) for 10 minutes.

Meanwhile, prepare the frangipane cream. Boil the milk and add the sugar to dissolve.

In a large bowl, cream together the cornstarch, egg, and egg yolks. Add the ground almonds and mix well. Pour in about 1 cup (8 fl. oz., 250 ml) of the hot milk, stirring to blend thoroughly.

Keep the milk remaining in the saucepan at a gentle simmer. Add the almond mixture and stir continuously. Boil for 4 minutes to cook the starch completely. Add the almond extract or liqueur.

Prepare the apricots. Boil the water and sugar together, then add the apricots and poach them for 12 minutes until tender. Drain and halve them, discarding the stones. The syrup can be retained to use on another occasion, if refrigerated.

To serve, turn out the rice mold onto a large, round platter. Decorate with halved apricots and sprinkle with Kirsch.

Serve the frangipane cream separately.

This dish can be served hot, warm, or chilled.

VARIATIONS

Peaches, nectarines, plums, pears, or pineapple can be used in place of the apricots. If served cold, the rice can be decorated with whipped cream, glacé cherries, *marrons glacés*, or angelica.

The frangipane cream can be used as a topping for an apricot flan. Arrange the fruit in a flan shell, then cover with the cream and bake for about 40 minutes. Sprinkle with toasted flaked almonds before serving.

Frangipane cream can also be served on its own or in a glass with fresh berry fruits.

SERVES 6-8

BREADS, CAKES, AND COOKIES
LES PAINS, GÂTEAUX, ET GALETTES

NORMANDY SHORTBREADS

LES SABLÉS DE CAEN

Normandy butter is justly famous, and these light and delicate little shortbreads owe their reputation to this. But they taste just as good made with any high-quality unsalted butter, as you are sure to discover.

5 oz. (155 g) unsalted butter, softened

⅓ cup (3 oz., 90 g) Demerara (raw) sugar,
ground to a powder

4 egg yolks, hard-boiled

2 cups (8 oz., 250 g) whole-wheat (wholemeal) flour

grated rind of 1 orange

juice of 1 lemon

2 tablespoons milk, to glaze

Beat together the butter and sugar (which must be very well powdered) until light and fluffy. Push the egg yolks through a sieve, then beat them into the mixture. Sift in the flour and beat in, then stir in the orange rind and lemon juice. Combine well to form a dough. Roll into a ball and refrigerate for 1 hour.

On a floured board, roll out the dough to a thickness of ¼ in. (6 mm). Cut out 4 circles, 6 in. (15 cm) in diameter. Mark each circle lightly into quarters with the back of a knife. Brush with a little milk to glaze.

Lay the circles on a greased baking sheet (tray) and bake in a preheated oven at 400°F (200°C) for about 15 minutes, taking care not to overcook.

Leave the shortbreads to cool before breaking into quarters and serving.

MAKES 16 SHORTBREADS

HONEY COOKIES FROM NIORT

LES BISCUITS AU MIEL DE NIORT

Niort, in the region of Poitou-Charentes, is 'twinned' with Wellingborough, in Britain. The spirit of 'entente' cordiale that the idea of twin towns engenders is very dear to me, linking as it does the country of my birth and the one that I have made my home.

5 oz. (155 g) butter

⅓ cup (4 oz., 125 g) honey

2 cups (8 oz., 250 g) whole-wheat (wholemeal) flour

1 teaspoon anise seeds

1 egg, beaten

½ teaspoon baking soda (bicarbonate of soda)

2 tablespoons warm milk

Put the butter and the honey in a pan and melt gently together.

Place the flour and anise seeds in a bowl. Gradually stir in the melted butter and honey, mixing to form a dough.

Add the egg to the bowl and mix in. Dissolve the baking soda in the warm milk, then add this. Stir and finally knead to form a smooth, firm paste. Leave to cool.

Form the cooled dough into a large sausage shape, about 2 in. (5 cm) in diameter. Cut diagonally into about 20 slices of equal thickness.

Place the honey rounds on a greased baking sheet (tray). Bake on the top shelf of a preheated oven at 350°F (180°C) for 15 to 20 minutes. Cool on a rack before serving.

MAKES 20 COOKIES

Pictured on previous pages: Normandy Shortbreads, and Honey Cookies from Niort
Pictured right: Cognac and Walnut Buns

COGNAC AND WALNUT BUNS

Les Tartisseaux Éléanore d'Aquitaine

You will find these little buns — a cross between brioches and doughnuts — in the town of La Rochelle. Most of the women in the area have their own version of this delightful snack, which can be served at any time of day with a glass of rosé or just a cup of coffee or chocolate.

4 cups (1 lb., 500 g) whole-wheat (wholemeal) flour

1 level teaspoon sea salt

3 eggs

1 heaped tablespoon (²/₃ oz., 20 g) fresh
compressed yeast

¹/₃ cup (3 fl. oz., 90 ml) warm water

¹/₄ cup (2 fl. oz., 60 ml) vegetable oil *or* melted butter

2 tablespoons cognac

¹/₂ cup (2 oz., 60 g) chopped walnuts

vegetable oil, for frying

Sift the flour and sea salt into a large bowl, tipping back any bran left in the sieve.

Beat the eggs, make a well in the flour, and gently stir in the eggs until well combined.

Cream the yeast with the water until smooth. Blend into the flour and egg until completely combined. Leave to ferment for 10 minutes.

Knead the mixture to a smooth dough. Roll into a ball, cover with a damp cloth, and leave to rise for 20 minutes.

Punch down the dough, add the oil or butter, and combine well. Cover the dough again and leave to rest for 15 minutes.

Punch the dough down again and knead in the cognac and walnuts. Cover and leave to rise to twice its volume. The resulting dough should be of a soft dropping consistency.

Form the dough into balls the size of an egg. Roll them in a light dusting of flour and leave to rest for 12 minutes.

Heat oil in a large saucepan — for safety, the oil should not come to more than halfway up the sides. Fry the buns, a few at a time, for 3 minutes, turning in the oil to ensure they cook evenly. Drain on paper towels.

Serve warm, with a compote of fruit.

SERVES 8

DRIED FRUIT BREAD

PAIN DE CAMPAGNE AUX FRUITS SECS

This fruit bread was served daily at the Buffet de la Halle at breakfast with café au lait and in the afternoon with good farm butter and a raspberry purée. It also makes a good base for 'pain perdu' and other such recipes.

1²/₃ cups (13 fl. oz., 405 ml) water, warmed to 77°F (25°C)

1 tablespoon (¹/₂ oz., 15 g) fresh compressed yeast

1 teaspoon molasses (dark treacle)

5 cups (1¹/₄ lbs., 625 g) whole-wheat (wholemeal) flour

1 teaspoon soy flour

1 teaspoon sea salt

¹/₃ cup (2 oz., 60 g) seedless raisins

¹/₃ cup (2 oz., 60 g) golden seedless raisins (sultanas)

¹/₃ cup (2 oz., 60 g) dried orange peel

1 teaspoon melted butter

¹/₃ cup (2 oz., 60 g) seeds of choice (you could use sunflower, poppy, sesame, *or* pumpkin seeds)

Mix the water, yeast, and molasses together in a cup. Set aside in a warm place for a few minutes to allow fermentation to begin.

Put the flour, soy flour, and salt in a large bowl and warm briefly in a low oven — to about 77°F (25°C). Remove and make a well in the center.

Pour the yeast solution into the well in the flour and knead to form a smooth dough. Roll into a ball, cover with an inverted bowl, and leave in a warm place to rise for 30 minutes.

Meanwhile, soak the raisins, sultanas, and orange peel in a little warm water to swell, then drain and pat dry.

Knock back the dough by pummeling it with the knuckles and knead in the dried fruit, butter, and seeds until mixed well. Roll the dough into a neat rectangle and place in a well-greased loaf pan. Cover and set aside to rise again for about 30 to 45 minutes — the dough should have risen well above the level of the pan.

Bake on the middle shelf of a preheated oven at 450°F (230°C) for 30 minutes. If the loaf is browning too fast, lower the heat to 400°F (200°C) after 10 minutes or so.

When the bread is cooked (it should sound hollow when tapped on the base), turn it out onto a rack to cool.

MAKES 1 LARGE LOAF

ALMOND BREAD WITH KIRSCH

LE PAIN D'AMANDES AU KIRSCH

Almonds are widely cultivated in the south of France, where they are often used to produce one of the most delicious bread-cakes ever invented — the famous 'pain d'amandes'. Many countries produce almonds and it is certainly the case that this nut is the most important in the world from a gastronomic point of view. It is used in a wide range of dishes, not just breads and cakes, and is the basis for liqueurs as well. Its flavor enhances and complements others like no other nut.

There are two types of almond: bitter and sweet. The bitter almond is an acquired taste and contains prussic acid, which makes this type of almond poisonous in large quantities. For this recipe I have used ground sweet almonds, the type most readily available.

7 oz. (225 g) butter, softened

¹/₂ cup (2 oz., 60 g) soft whole-wheat (wholemeal) flour

²/₃ cup (5 oz., 155 g) Demerara (raw) sugar, ground to a powder

1 cup (4 oz., 125 g) ground almonds

3 eggs, beaten

pinch of sea salt

¹/₃ cup (3 fl. oz., 90 ml) Kirsch

Prepare a 9-in. (22.5-cm) cake pan, 2 in. (5 cm) deep — grease with 1 oz. (30 g) butter, then line with parchment or baking paper and grease that with a further 1 oz. (30 g) butter. Sprinkle on 1 tablespoon flour to coat the butter.

Beat the remaining butter and the sugar together until pale and fluffy. Add the ground almonds and flour. Beat well.

Blend the eggs into the mixture until completely smooth, then add the salt and Kirsch. Mix all the ingredients together thoroughly.

Pour this mixture into the prepared pan and smooth the top. Bake in a preheated oven at 375°F (190°C) for 40 minutes.

Turn the bread out onto a cooling rack. When cool, sprinkle with Kirsch. Wrap in foil and keep for 2 days before eating.

MAKES 1 SMALL LOAF

Pictured opposite: Dried Fruit Bread

Country Whole-Wheat Bread

Le Pain Bis de Campagne

This is the bread my grandmother used to bake in the communal village oven twice a week when I was a child. It can be produced from start to finish in 1½ hours. You can either bake it in two 1-lb. (500-g) loaf pans or make it into two loaves of whatever shape you like. My grandmother's loaves were round, but you could plait yours, or make a cottage loaf. If making a loaf without a pan, prove it in a bread basket of the appropriate shape lined with a piece of coarse material. Transfer the loaves to a greased baking sheet (tray) just before baking.

5 cups (1¼ lb., 625 g) whole-wheat (wholemeal) flour

2 tablespoons sea salt

1 teaspoon molasses (black treacle) *or* honey

1 teaspoon each of sesame seeds, sunflower seeds, rolled porridge oats, and ground hazelnuts *or* ground peanuts

1 teaspoon soy flour

2 tablespoons (1 oz., 30 g) compressed fresh yeast

13 fl. oz. (405 ml) water

juice of ¼ lemon

2 oz. (60 g) hard vegetable fat, for greasing

Put the flour in a heap on a large pastry board and make a well in the top. In the well, place the salt, molasses or honey, the seeds, rolled oats, nuts, and soy flour.

In a cup, blend the yeast with about ½ cup (4 fl. oz., 125 ml) water, then pour into the well of flour. Sprinkle a little flour on top and leave for 10 minutes until slightly foamy.

Warm the rest of the water to 74°F (23°C) and add this to the yeast mixture in the well of flour. Gradually mix all the flour and water together into a dough and knead well. Roll into a ball and leave covered by a large inverted bowl or in a plastic bag for 30 minutes.

'Punch down' the dough, add the lemon juice and knead well. Shape the mixture into two balls. Elongate a ball of dough by pulling gently at each end, then fold the ends into the middle to make a neat rectangular shape. Repeat with the other ball.

Grease two loaf pans with the vegetable fat, then place the loaves, folded sides downwards, in the pans. Alternatively, shape into the type of loaf you prefer. Leave to rise for 30 minutes in a warm place. Bake in a preheated oven at 425°F (220°C) for 30 minutes. Remove the loaves from the pans and cool on racks.

MAKES TWO 14-OZ. (435-G) LOAVES

Breakfast Rolls

Les Petits Pains de Déjeuner

The best way to learn how to make bread is by preparing a dough suitable for small rolls. What you learn to do well with small amounts of dough can easily be adapted to larger quantities.

4 cups (1 lb., 500 g) strong whole-wheat (wholemeal) flour

2 tablespoons (1 oz., 30 g) compressed fresh yeast

9 fl. oz. (280 ml) water

1 teaspoon Demerara (raw) sugar

2 tablespoons low-fat milk powder

4 oz. (125 g) hard vegetable fat

1 teaspoon sea salt

¼ cup (2 fl. oz., 60 ml) milk, for glazing

Reserve 1 tablespoon flour. Place the rest in a heap on a large pastry board. Make a well in the center. Crumble the yeast into one-third of the water and stir until well mixed, then pour into the well and sprinkle with the reserved flour, sugar, and milk powder. Leave to ferment for 12 minutes.

Heat the remaining water to 80°F (27°C) (if you are unsure, use a cooking thermometer to check the temperature). Add this water to the yeast mixture in the well of flour and gradually draw all the flour into the liquid until blended thoroughly (use a fork or your fingers to do this).

Knead the dough well, then roll it into a ball. Cover the dough with an inverted bowl or place in a plastic bag to retain the temperature of the dough. Leave for 40 minutes.

When the dough has rested and risen for 40 minutes, 'punch down' by pummeling with the knuckles. Reshape it into a ball and scatter the top with half the vegetable fat, cut into small pieces.

Leave the dough to rise again for 10 minutes, then knead to blend in the fat. Shape into a ball again and sprinkle the top with salt.

Divide the dough into 18 equal-sized pieces. Roll each one into a neat ball.

Grease a baking sheet (tray) with the rest of the vegetable fat and arrange the rolls on it. Brush the rolls with a little milk and leave to rise for a further 20 to 25 minutes in a warm place.

Preheat the oven to 425°F (220°C) and bake the rolls on the middle shelf for 15 to 20 minutes.

Serve warm or cold with fresh butter.

MAKES 18 ROLLS

Pictured above right: Cornmeal Bread

CORNMEAL BREAD

LE PAIN AU MAÏS

Bread made with cornmeal needs the addition of wheat flour, otherwise it will be too heavy. Corn was only introduced into France in the 16th century, but now it is grown extensively in all regions. In many places, corn is used more as animal fodder than as a food for people, but a loaf such as this one, where corn and wheat are correctly balanced to produce a substantial, flavorsome bread, makes a very pleasant change.

1 cup (5 oz., 155 g) cornmeal

1 cup (8 fl. oz., 250 ml) boiling water

2 teaspoons sea salt

1 tablespoon honey

2 tablespoons corn oil

2 tablespoons (1 oz., 30 g) compressed fresh yeast

1 teaspoon Demerara (raw) sugar

2/3 cup (5 fl. oz., 155 ml) tepid water

4 1/2 cups (1 lb. 2 oz., 560 g) whole-wheat (wholemeal) flour

1 oz. (30 g) hard vegetable fat, for greasing

milk, to glaze

Put the cornmeal in a large bowl. Pour over the boiling water and leave to soak for 15 minutes. Stir in the salt, honey, and oil.

Place the yeast and sugar in a cup. Stir in the tepid water and add a pinch of flour, then leave to ferment for 15 minutes, by which time the mixture should be foamy.

Stir the yeast ferment into the cornmeal. Reserve ½ cup (2 oz., 60 g) flour. Add the rest to the cornmeal mixture and stir well.

Knead the mixture to a smooth dough on a large, floured pastry board. Knead very well, punching and stretching the dough to really elasticate the gluten in the whole-wheat flour (the cornmeal is low in gluten).

Roll the dough into a ball, cover with an inverted bowl, and leave to rise for 45 minutes.

'Punch down' the dough by pummeling with the knuckles. Knead again, then shape it into a ball.

Grease a large round loaf pan with vegetable fat. Place the dough in the pan, brush with a little milk, and leave to rise again, in a warm place, until the dough has risen to the top of the pan in a dome shape. Sprinkle with the reserved flour.

Bake in a preheated oven at 400°F (200°C) for 35 minutes, until golden-brown and, when tapped on the base, has a hollow sound.

Cool on a rack.

Note: This loaf freezes well, as do many breads, but it should be wrapped up well before freezing and should not be refrozen once defrosted. Even just wrapped in plastic and stored in a bread box, this loaf will keep well for several days. The loaf can also be baked in a round pan and sliced cake-like, if preferred.

MAKES A 2-LB. (1-KG) LOAF

BAKED LEMONY YEAST CAKES

LES NAPOLÉONS D'OR

When Napoleon's son was born in Rome, the antecedents of these little cakes were baked in celebration. Their origin is thought to be Bohemian, and they are good served in the manner traditional to that region, with a brandied custard sauce and stewed apricots. Baked crisp and golden, to resemble Napoleon's francs, they are a treasure indeed.

1 tablespoon (1/2 oz., 15 g) fresh compressed yeast

1/4 cup (2 fl. oz., 60 ml) lukewarm water

1/4 cup (2 oz., 60 g) sugar

2 1/2 cups (10 oz., 310 g) whole-wheat (wholemeal) flour

1/4 cup (1 oz., 30 g) cornstarch (cornflour)

1/4 teaspoon sea salt

1 egg, beaten

1/2 cup (4 fl. oz., 125 ml) buttermilk

1/4 cup (2 oz., 60 g) melted butter

grated rind of 1 lemon

1 tablespoon vegetable oil

extra melted butter, to glaze

Dissolve the yeast in the water. Add the sugar and leave to ferment for 15 minutes.

Sift together the flour, cornstarch, and salt in a bowl, then place in a low oven briefly to warm. Remove and make a well in the center.

Pour the yeast mixture into the well and knead. Add the combined egg, buttermilk and butter, and knead thoroughly to form a smooth dough. Gather into a ball, cover with a damp cloth, and leave to rise in a warm place for 1 hour.

'Punch down' the dough and knead in the lemon rind. Leave to rest for 15 minutes.

Roll the dough out to a thickness of 1/2 in. (1 cm). Use a glass or cookie cutter to cut out 1-in. (2.5-cm) rounds.

Brush the sides of each round with oil and lay them not too close together on a greased baking sheet (tray) (the oil will allow the rounds to be separated after baking). Brush the tops with melted butter. Leave to rise for 20 minutes.

Place in an oven preheated at 400°F (200°C) for 15 minutes. Remove from the oven and lower the heat to 350°F (180°C). Brush the tops again with melted butter and return to the oven to cook for a further 10 to 15 minutes, until crisp and golden.

Serve with a custard sauce flavored with apricot brandy, and apricots poached until tender in a little honey and vermouth.

SERVES 4

FLEMISH WAFFLES

LES GAUFRES DE LILLE

True French waffles are made in beautifully decorated irons, many of which have been handed down through the generations. But this recipe tastes equally good freshly cooked in the gridded version that is more familiar outside of France.

1 tablespoon (1/2 oz., 15 g) fresh compressed yeast

2/3 cup (5 fl. oz., 155 ml) warm milk

2 1/2 cups (10 oz., 300 g) whole-wheat (wholemeal) flour

1/2 teaspoon sea salt

2 eggs, beaten

1 teaspoon Demerara (raw) sugar, ground to a powder

In a cup, mix the yeast with the warm milk. In a bowl, mix together the flour and salt. Make a well and pour in the eggs. Add the yeast mixture and sugar and beat everything well to form a smooth batter. Leave to ferment for 30 minutes, then beat again.

Lightly grease a waffle iron and heat well. Pour a little of the batter in — about 1/4 cup (2 fl. oz., 60 ml) per waffle — close the iron, and cook for about 5 minutes. Remove from the waffle iron and keep warm. Repeat the process until the batter is all used. Serve hot, drizzled with a little clear honey.

MAKES 12 WAFFLES

Pictured opposite: Baked Lemony Yeast Cakes

SWEET BREAD LOAF

....

LE PAIN BÉNIT

My grandmother's special Sunday bread, decorated with dried fruits and almonds, was always a treat.

3 tablespoons (1½ oz., 45 g) compressed fresh yeast

2½ cups (1 imp. pint, 625 ml) milk

7 cups (1¾ lb., 750 g) strong whole-wheat (wholemeal) flour

scant ⅓ cup (2½ oz., 75 g) Demerara (raw) sugar

3 tablespoons sea salt

1 teaspoon honey

4 oz. (125 g) butter, softened

juice of ¼ lemon

½ cup (3 oz., 90 g) glacé cherries, halved

⅔ cup (3 oz., 90 g) citrus peel

½ cup (3 oz., 90 g) chopped angelica

½ cup (2 oz., 60 g) slivered almonds

1 oz. (30 g) vegetable fat, for greasing

1 egg, beaten, to glaze

extra 2 tablespoons milk, to glaze

3 tablespoons (2 oz., 60 g) clear honey, to glaze

Heat the milk to 77°F (25°C) in a saucepan. Place the yeast in a bowl and pour in the warmed milk, dispersing the yeast well. Sprinkle with 2 tablespoons flour and leave for 12 minutes.

Put the remaining flour in a large bowl and make a well in the top. Sift the sugar and salt together into the well. Add the fermented yeast and honey and beat together into a dough. Knead well. Roll into a ball. Dot the top of the dough with the butter, cover with an inverted bowl, and leave to rise for 45 minutes.

Knead the dough again so the butter is well blended. Add the lemon juice and half of the cherries, peel, angelica, and almonds. Knead the dough quickly to mix them in, then cover and leave to rise for 20 minutes. (The temperature of your dough should be 77°–84°F (25°–29°C).)

Divide the dough into three equal parts. Roll each part into a pointed sausage shape, about 9 in. (22.5 cm) long. Join the three strands together at one end and plait into a neat loaf, joining the strands together at the other end.

Grease a baking sheet (tray) with vegetable fat and place the loaf on it. Mix the egg and milk together and brush over the loaf. Leave to rise for 35 to 40 minutes; the loaf will double in size.

Glaze the loaf with egg and milk again. Bake for 35 minutes in a preheated oven at 400°F (200°C). Towards the end of the cooking, heat the honey gently and, as soon as the loaf is removed from the oven, brush it with melted honey and decorate the top with the rest of the dried fruit and almonds.

MAKES A 3-LB. (1.5-KG) PLAITED LOAF

BRIOCHE

LE PAIN BRIOCHÉ

The oft-quoted phrase of Marie-Antoinette, 'Let them eat cake', about the shortage of bread in France just before the Revolution is, in fact, a misquote. What she really said was, 'If the people are short of bread, give them brioche.' This is because the shortage of flour could be supplemented by the addition of milk and eggs.

The French certainly love their bread, and it was the shortage of flour — a ridiculous situation in a cereal-rich country like France — that finally precipitated the French Revolution. But these days, every French person can dunk their brioche into their hot chocolate for breakfast, as I do. There is no better breakfast, to my mind!

An enriched dough, such as brioche, needs extra help to make it good and light. For this reason a mixture of flour, water, and yeast is given time to ferment before being added to the main ingredients. This gets the yeast off to a flying start. A 'baker's ferment', as this first mixture is called, looks rather like very thin pancake batter, but the action of the yeast makes it bubble and boil, hence the name 'ferment'.

1/2 cup (4 fl. oz., 125 ml) mixed milk and water

1 tablespoon (1/2 oz., 15 g) fresh compressed yeast

4 1/2 cups (1 lb. 2 oz., 560 g) whole-wheat (wholemeal) flour, slightly warmed

2 tablespoons Demerara (raw) sugar

1 tablespoon sea salt

4—5 eggs, beaten

6 oz. (185 g) butter, softened

2 oz. (60 g) hard vegetable fat, for greasing

extra milk, to glaze

Heat the milk and water to 77°F (25°C) and stir half into the yeast. Blend well and stir into a quarter of the flour, in a bowl. Leave to ferment for 15 to 20 minutes, by which time the mixture should have doubled in volume.

Meanwhile, place the remaining flour on a large pastry board and make a well in the top. Put the sugar and salt in the well, then pour in the remaining half of the warm milk and water to dissolve slightly.

Add some of the beaten egg. Begin drawing the flour into the liquids, using a fork or your fingers and adding more egg if the mixture seems to be getting stiff. Mix the dough for a good 10 minutes to achieve a soft, pliable texture — 'plastic', as it is known in culinary terms.

Add the softened butter and knead well. (This can be done in an electric mixer with a dough hook, if preferred.)

Add the ferment, either by hand or in the mixer, making sure it is completely kneaded into the dough. Put the dough in a clean bowl, cover with a clean cloth, dust with a little flour, and leave to rise for 1½ to 2 hours.

Grease a loaf pan or a large brioche pan with vegetable fat and also grease 12 small, fluted brioche molds; alternatively, make a second loaf.

Weigh out 1 lb. (500 g) of dough and shape to fit the pan. Brush the top with milk and leave for a further 35 to 45 minutes in a warm place, until it has risen above the edge of the pan.

Divide the remaining dough into 12 equal pieces, then break off about a quarter of each piece. Place the larger pieces of dough in the brioche molds and make a dent in their tops. Shape the smaller pieces into pear shapes and place these on top of the larger pieces so that the pointed end fits into the dent — like miniature cottage loaves.

Brush the little buns with milk (mixed with any leftover egg) to glaze. Leave to rise in a warm place for 20 minutes.

Preheat the oven to 400°C (200°F). Bake the buns for 15 to 20 minutes and the loaf for 35 minutes. The heat can be lowered to 375°C (190°F) once the buns have been removed if the top of the bread is getting too brown.

Remove the buns and bread from their pans and cool on racks.

Note: If you bake the loaf in a large brioche pan, follow the shaping instructions for the little brioches to make the traditional 'cottage' top.

MAKES A 1-LB. (500-G) LOAF
AND 12 SMALL BUNS,
OR TWO 1-LB. (500-G) LOAVES

Pictured left: Sweet Bread Loaf

Honey Bread with Anise Seeds

Le Pain d'épices

Once a year the typically French Amiens Fair is the place to sample dozens of varieties of the wonderful 'pain d'épice' at the stalls that line the fairground.
This honey bread, flavored with spices, is not as sweet as you might imagine. Eat it with lashings of butter.

2 cups (8 oz., 250 g) whole-wheat (wholemeal) flour

2 cups (8 oz., 250 g) rye flour

1/4 teaspoon each of ground cloves, ground cinnamon, ground ginger, and anise seeds

1 level teaspoon cream of tartar

2 eggs, beaten

1 level teaspoon baking soda (bicarbonate of soda)

1/2 cup (4 fl. oz., 125 ml) warm milk

2 oz. (60 g) hard vegetable fat, for greasing

Glaze
1/2 cup (4 oz., 125 g) Demerara (raw) sugar

3 tablespoons milk

3 tablespoons water

In a saucepan, heat the honey until almost boiling. Mix the whole-wheat and rye flours together in a large bowl. Stir in the spices and cream of tartar.

Bring the honey to the boil, pour it over the flour, and beat hard to form a dough. Stir in the eggs. Dissolve the baking soda in the milk and blend into the dough.

Grease 2 loaf tins with vegetable fat. Pour in the dough and leave to rest for 1 hour.

Place on the middle shelf of a preheated oven and bake at 400°F (200°C) for 20 minutes, then reduce heat to 350°F (180°C) and bake for a further 20 minutes.

Meanwhile, boil the sugar, milk, and water together in a pan for 5 to 8 minutes to form a thick syrup. As soon as you remove the loaves from the oven, brush their tops with this syrup to form a glaze. Cool the bread on a rack.

Variations
The top of the bread can be decorated with citrus peel, glacé cherries, or angelica after baking.

Note: Leave the loaves in an airtight tin for 2 days before cutting so the flavors can develop.

MAKES 2 SMALL LOAVES

Rye Bread with Caraway Seeds

Le Pain au Carvi

Rye comes second to wheat in popularity as a breadmaking grain. It has a very distinctive, slightly sour taste, which many people find appealing but which might need to be mellowed with wheat flour if you have not tried it before.
Many traditional recipes blend the two flours, 'stretching' the more scarce and luxurious wheat flour. Rye bread also keeps better than bread made with wheat flour alone.
The aromatic flavor of caraway seeds goes particularly well with rye bread.

2 tablespoons (1 oz., 30 g) fresh compressed yeast

2 1/2 cups (1 imp. pint, 625 ml) water

2 cups (8 oz., 250 g) rye flour

6 cups (1 1/2 lbs., 750 g) whole-wheat (wholemeal) flour

3 tablespoons sea salt

1 tablespoon malt extract

1 teaspoon caraway seeds

1 oz. (30 g) hard vegetable fat, for greasing

milk, to glaze

Warm the water to 77°F (25°C) and blend the yeast with half of it. Place the rye flour in a large bowl and stir in the yeast liquid. Leave covered for 1 hour to ferment.

Place the wheat flour in a large bowl and make a well in the center. Add the salt and malt extract, then stir in the rest of the water. Add half the caraway seeds and mix well to form a stiff dough.

When the ferment has doubled in size, blend it into the dough. Knead by hand or with an electric mixer fitted with a dough hook for 5 minutes. Roll the dough into a ball, cover with a cloth or an inverted bowl, and leave to rise for 40 minutes.

Lightly grease a rectangular loaf pan or a baking sheet (tray) with vegetable fat. Shape the dough into a loaf accordingly. Brush with a little milk and sprinkle with the remaining caraway seeds. Leave to rise for a further 30 minutes.

Bake in a preheated oven at 425°F (220°C) for 30 minutes. When golden-brown and hollow-sounding when tapped on its base, turn the loaf out onto a cooling rack.

MAKES 1 LARGE LOAF

Pictured opposite: Honey Bread with Anise Seeds

CRÊPES

Brittany is the home of the crêpe, and every little village has its crêperie serving these inexpensive and delicious items with every imaginable filling, from seafood to Grand Marnier liqueur. The savory version is usually made with buckwheat flour, and is then called a 'galette'. Galettes are substantial and filling, with a nutty flavour in their own right. If you can find buckwheat flour, this version of a crêpe is well worth a try.

2 eggs, beaten

1¼ cups (10 fl. oz., 310 ml) milk

1 cup (4 oz., 125 g) whole-wheat (wholemeal) flour

pinch of sea salt

vegetable oil, for frying

Mix the eggs and milk together. Sift the flour and salt into a bowl. Stir the egg mixture in to make a smooth, lump-free batter.

Heat a little oil in a 6-in. (15-cm) crêpe pan and pour in a quarter of the batter. Cook the crêpe evenly on both sides until golden-brown, then set aside. Repeat until you have four neat, even-sized crêpes and use as required.

MAKES 4

YEASTED PANCAKES WITH MIRABELLES

LES CRÊPETTES AUX MIRABELLES

This recipe uses a yeast base, which produces pancakes similar to crumpets or English muffins. They are sandwiched together with a mixture of mirabelles (plums) flavored with port and sweetened fresh cheese.

YEASTED PANCAKES

2 tablespoons (1 oz., 30 g) fresh yeast

¼ cup (2 fl. oz., 60 ml) warm milk

4 cups (1 lb., 500 g) whole-wheat (wholemeal) flour

¼ teaspoon sea salt

¼ teaspoon sugar

½ teaspoon cinnamon

2 eggs, beaten

1¼ cups (10 fl. oz., 310 ml) buttermilk

FILLING

8 oz. (250 g) mirabelles (cherry plums), halved and pitted

¼ cup (2 fl. oz., 60 ml) port

3 tablespoons (2 oz., 60 g) honey

½ teaspoon cornflour

6 oz. (185 g) curd cheese

¼ cup (2 fl. oz., 60 ml) heavy cream, whipped

2 egg whites, whisked to form firm peaks

Crumble the yeast into the warm milk and blend until smooth.

In a bowl, mix together the flour, salt, sugar, and cinnamon. Make a well in the center and pour in the yeast mixture. Cover with a little flour and leave to ferment for 15 minutes. Stir in the eggs and buttermilk and mix to a smooth batter.

Poach the mirabelles in the port and honey until soft. Strain off a little of the juice and mix with the cornflour, then return this to the plums and heat to thicken. Set aside.

Beat together the cheese, cream, and whisked egg whites. Set aside.

Oil a large skillet or frying pan and drop in spoonfuls of batter, six at a time, to make small pancakes. Cook on one side until golden and risen, then turn over and cook the other side. Drain on paper towels. Repeat until batter is used up.

To serve, place a spoonful of fruit mixture onto half the quantity of pancakes. Spoon a little of the cheese mixture over, cover with one of the remaining pancakes and press down firmly on one side. Sift sugar over before serving if desired.

SERVES 4

Pictured right: Apricot Biscuits

APRICOT BISCUITS

LES PETITS GÂTEAUX À L'ABRICOT

These tasty biscuits (scones) are so simple, they can even be made by children as their very own contribution to the meal.

4 cups (1 lb., 500 g) wholemeal flour

2 tablespoons (1 oz., 30 g) baking powder

pinch of sea salt

2 oz. (60 g) butter

1 egg, beaten

1 cup (8 fl. oz., 250 ml) sour cream

scant ¼ cup (2 oz., 60 g) apricot jelly (jam)

milk *or* egg, to glaze

Mix together the flour, baking powder, and salt in a bowl. Rub in the butter with your fingertips to make a crumb-like consistency.

In a separate bowl, beat together the egg, sour cream, and jelly until well mixed. Stir into the flour mixture for a soft dough.

Form the dough into a sausage shape about 2 in. (5 cm) in diameter and cut into slices ½ in. (1 cm) thick. Lay these on a greased baking sheet (tray) and brush with a milk or egg wash. Leave to rest for 10 minutes.

Bake the biscuits on the middle shelf of a preheated oven at 425°F (220°C) for 8 to 10 minutes. Cool slightly on a rack before serving.

MAKES 8 BISCUITS

PARISIAN CIGARETTES

CIGARETTES PARISIENNES

Don't worry — I am not advocating cooking with Gauloises! Parisian cigarettes in this context are delicate 'langue de chat' biscuits, rolled while still warm. They can be shaped in other ways, too; for example, a fluted cup shape can be used to hold a scoop of sorbet for a charming dinner party dessert. This recipe calls for confectioner's (icing) sugar, which is not a wholefood, but these cookies (biscuits) are consumed in small quantities on special occasions, so I think we can make an allowance to achieve the correct texture and flavor.

6 oz. (185 g) butter, softened
1 cup (5 oz., 155 g) confectioner's (icing) sugar
6 egg whites
¼ cup (2 oz., 60 g) Demerara (raw) sugar, ground to a powder
1 cup (4 oz., 125 g) whole-wheat (wholemeal) flour
⅔ cup (5 fl. oz., 155 ml) light cream

Cream together the butter and confectioner's (icing) sugar until light and fluffy.

In another bowl, whisk the egg whites until stiff, then fold in the raw sugar and whisk again. Fold into the butter mixture, then fold in the flour and cream to form a light, smooth batter.

Fit a pastry bag with a small plain tip (nozzle) and pipe dots of batter onto a greased and lightly floured baking sheet (tray). Leave about 1½ in. (4 cm) around each of the dots, as the mixture will spread while cooking.

Bake in a preheated oven at 425°F (220°C) for 6 to 8 minutes, until golden all over and lightly browned at the edges.

Shape the cookies into cigarette shapes around the handle of a wooden spoon (or into whatever shape you require) as soon as they are cool enough for you to handle them. Or leave them flat, if you prefer. They will firm and crisp as they cool.

MAKES ABOUT 50 COOKIES

SPICE AND HONEY BARS

LES BISCUITS DE CRÉCY AUX ÉPICES

This recipe from the Flemish region of France demonstrates the true use of the word biscuit, or 'bis cuit' — meaning twice cooked.

4 cups (1 lb., 500 g) whole-wheat (wholemeal) flour
½ cup (2 oz., 60 g) ground almonds
1 teaspoon ground ginger
1 teaspoon mixed spice
1 teaspoon anise seeds
8 oz. (250 g) butter *or* vegetable margarine
⅔ cup (8 oz., 250 g) honey, warmed
½ teaspoon baking soda (bicarbonate of soda)
2 tablespoons warmed milk *or* water

Stir together the flour, almonds, ginger, mixed spice, and anise seeds in a bowl. Rub in the butter or margarine with your fingertips to make a breadcrumb-like consistency.

Stir in the warmed honey. Dissolve the baking soda in the milk or water and add this too. Mix well together to form a rich, pourable dough.

Pour the dough into a greased baking pan, 15 x 8 in. (37.5 x 20 cm) and 2 in. (5 cm) deep. Bake in a preheated oven at 400°F (200°C) for 15 to 20 minutes, until starting to turn golden.

Remove the pan from the oven. Cut the dough into 16 bars without removing from the pan. Return to the oven and continue cooking for a further 15 minutes.

Allow to cool in the pan before taking out and separating the bars.

MAKES 16 BARS

Pictured opposite: Parisian Cigarettes

SEMI-SWEET BUTTER CRACKERS

....

LES CRAQUELINS DE SAINT QUENTIN

This is an old French recipe, dating from the days of Jeanne d'Arc, the Maid of Orleans. These crisp little crackers are as simple to make as they are delicious.

4 oz. (125 g) butter

2 cups (8 oz., 250 g) whole-wheat (wholemeal) flour

2 egg yolks

1/2 cup (4 fl. oz., 125 ml) milk

good pinch of sea salt

egg, beaten, to glaze

2 tablespoons Demerara (raw) sugar

Cream together the butter and flour, then beat in the egg yolks, milk, and salt to make a dough. Cover and refrigerate for 2 hours.

Dust a board with flour and roll out the dough to a thickness of ¼ inch (6 mm). Use a cookie cutter to cut out circles 2 in. (5 cm) in diameter.

Grease and lightly flour a baking sheet (tray) and lay the circles of dough on it. Brush with egg wash and bake in a preheated oven at 450°F (230°C) for 8 to 10 minutes, or until golden.

Remove the baking sheet (tray) from the oven and brush the crackers with egg wash again, then sprinkle with sugar. Return to the oven for a further 3 minutes. Cool on a rack before serving.

MAKES 18 CRACKERS

FRENCH FILLED CROISSANTS

....

LES CROISSANTS CONIL

Here are the best croissants in the world – or so our customers say!

PASTRY

4 cups (1 lb., 500 g) strong whole-wheat (wholemeal) flour

1/2 teaspoon sea salt

1 1/2 oz. (45 g) Demerara (raw) sugar

1 tablespoon (1/2 oz., 15 g) compressed fresh yeast

1 cup (8 fl. oz., 250 ml) milk

1 egg, beaten

12 oz. (375 g) butter

FILLING

4 oz. (125 g) butter

2 eggs, beaten

1/2 cup (2 oz., 60 g) ground almonds

1/2 cup (2 oz., 60 g) ground, toasted peanuts

1/2 cup (2 oz., 60 g) whole-wheat (wholemeal) flour

1/2 cup (4 oz., 125 g) Demerara (raw) sugar, ground to a powder

2 tablespoons dark rum

GLAZE

1 egg, beaten

2 tablespoons milk

2 tablespoons apricot jelly (jam), warmed (optional)

1/2 cup (2 oz., 60 g) slivered almonds

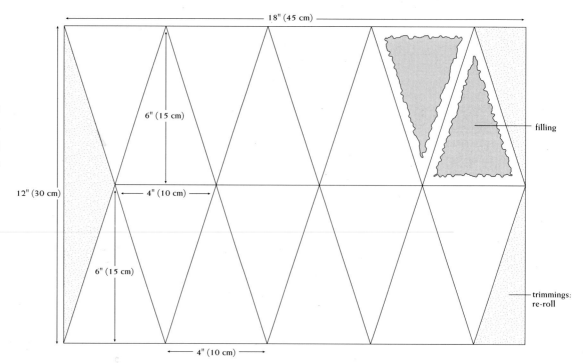

To make the pastry, sift the flour and salt together in a bowl. Stir in the sugar.

In a cup, stir the yeast into the milk, which has been warmed to 77°C (25°C). Blend in the egg, then mix into the flour to form a dough. Knead the dough thoroughly, roll into a ball, and place in a plastic bag to rise for 10 minutes.

'Punch down' the dough by pummeling it with the knuckles to get rid of the air. Roll into a ball again and let stand.

Shape the butter into a 6-in. (15-cm) square. Chill for 10 minutes.

Roll the dough into a 12-in. (30-cm) square. Place the butter on top of the dough and fold the edges of the dough over it to cover it completely.

Dust with flour and roll the dough out into a rectangle about 18 x 9 in. (45 x 22.5 cm). Fold the two long sides to meet in the middle of the dough, then fold in half at the center like a book. Chill for 15 minutes in the refrigerator.

Repeat the rolling and folding process, then refrigerate while you prepare the filling.

Combine all the filling ingredients, beating until light and fluffy.

Roll out the dough to make an 18 x 12-in. (45 x

30-cm) rectangle. Cut out triangles that are 4 in. (10 cm) at the base and 6 in. (15 cm) from base to tip (see diagram). This should make 16 triangles, leaving trimmings at either end of the rectangle. Re-roll these trimmings and cut a further 2 triangles.

Spread a little of the filling onto each triangle, to within ¼ in. (6 mm) of the edges. Roll the triangles up carefully from the base to the point, then press the edges to seal in the filling. Curve the roll into the traditional crescent shape, with the curved ends pointing away from the tip of the triangle.

Brush the croissants with a mixture of egg and milk. Place on a lightly greased baking sheet (tray), cover with loose plastic wrap, and leave to rise for 20 minutes.

Preheat the oven to 425°F (220°C) and bake the croissants for 15 to 20 minutes.

As soon as the croissants are removed from the oven, brush with a little beaten egg, milk, or warmed apricot jam, and sprinkle with almonds.

MAKES 18 CROISSANTS

Pictured above: Semi-sweet Butter Crackers
Pictured left: cutting guide for making croissants

SHORTCRUST PASTRY

PÂTE BRISÉE

This pastry is the basis for any quiche, and there are so many varieties of traditional French quiche: Quiche Savoyarde is filled with boiled, diced potatoes and the creamy custard flavored with garlic; Quiche Boulonnaise is a simple custard flavored with onions and cheese; Quiche Niçoise is filled with a custard mixed with green or string beans, tomatoes, black olives, and onions.

2 cups (8 oz., 250 g) whole-wheat (wholemeal) flour

4 oz. (125 g) margarine

1 egg, beaten

2 tablespoons water

pinch of sea salt

Sift the flour into a large bowl or onto a large pastry board. Rub the butter into the flour to form a crumbly consistency.

Beat the egg, water, and salt together in a separate bowl. Pour this mixture slowly into the flour and butter. Knead to form a dough. This should take about 1 minute.

Roll the dough into a ball, cover with plastic wrap, and allow to rest for 30 minutes.

Use as required.

SWEET SHORTCRUST PASTRY

PÂTE SUCRÉE

This light, sweet pastry bakes to a biscuit-like crispness that complements any fruity or creamy filling. If the filling is very juicy, you can paint the interior of the baked pastry case with gently melted (not boiled!) unsweetened dark chocolate. This ensures that the pastry doesn't absorb any liquid but remains dry and crisp during the cooking process.

2 cups (8 oz., 250 g) whole-wheat (wholemeal) flour

1 pinch of mixed spice

4 oz. (125 g) butter

2 tablespoons Demerara (raw) sugar, ground to a powder

1 tablespoon vegetable oil

1 egg, beaten

Sift the flour into a large bowl. Add the spices and stir together. Rub in the butter to form a breadcrumb-like consistency.

Stir in the sugar, oil, and egg to make a firm batter. Only knead until evenly combined.

Roll the dough into a ball, cover with plastic wrap, and refrigerate for 30 minutes.

Use as required.

CHOUX PASTRY

PÂTE À CHOUX

Once you have discovered just how easy it is to make choux pastry, you will be amazed by its versatility.

½ cup (4 fl. oz., 125 ml) water

2 oz. (60 g) butter

1 cup (4 oz., 125 g) whole-wheat (wholemeal) flour

3 small eggs, beaten

sea salt and freshly ground black pepper

Put the water and butter in a large saucepan and heat until the fat melts and the water boils.

Tip in all the flour at once, very quickly, and stir fast to blend together. Keep stirring over the heat until the mixture forms a smooth, very thick paste that comes away cleanly from the sides of the pan in a solid mass. Remove from the heat and cool for 4 minutes.

Gradually beat in the eggs until the paste forms a thick dropping consistency. Season lightly with salt and pepper.

Use as required.

Pictured left: Apple Flan, Normandy Style, using Sweet Shortcrust Pastry

PUFF PASTRY

PÂTE FEUILLETÉE

Here I've supplied my recipe for puff pastry, but if you don't have a lot of time, a package of shop-bought puff pastry will suffice.

2 cups (8 oz., 250 g) whole-wheat (wholemeal) bread flour

pinch of sea salt

8 oz. (250 g) butter

½ cup (4 fl. oz., 125 ml) water

1 tablespoon lemon juice

Sift the flour and salt into a large bowl. Reserve the bran for some other dish.

Rub a quarter of the butter into the flour. Make a well in the mixture and add the water and lemon juice then knead the mixture to a dough and roll into a ball.

Slash the top of the dough in a cross-wise pattern, cover with a damp cloth, and allow to rest for 30 minutes.

Meanwhile, knead the remaining butter until it is the same consistency as the pastry dough, then roll it out on a floured board to a neat rectangle, about ⅛ in. (3 mm) thick. You will need to flour the butter, the rolling pin, and the board very carefully so that the butter does not stick.

Roll out the dough to the same thickness as the butter. Place the butter on top of the dough and fold the two layers three times. Roll again into a rectangle, fold into three again, then rest the dough for 20 minutes.

Repeat this procedure twice more, then wrap in plastic wrap and chill until needed.

Use as required.

Sauces and Dressings
Les Coulis et Compotes

BASIC MAYONNAISE

MAYONNAISE

There is still an air of mystery about mayonnaise-making. It has a reputation for being difficult yet, if you follow the instructions, it is really very simple. Mayonnaise is an emulsion — that is, two liquids that cannot combine completely are whisked together so that one is suspended in the other. With mayonnaise, the mixing is rather special, however, because whisking increases the volume and the egg yolks can miraculously absorb far more than their own volume in oil, thus binding and thickening the emulsion so that it remains thick. Mayonnaise is always a cold sauce — heating will cook the eggs, ruining the emulsion.

4 egg yolks
1 teaspoon Dijon *or* French mustard
1/2 teaspoon sea salt
large pinch freshly ground pepper
1¹/4 cups (10 fl. oz., 310 ml) walnut *or* olive oil
juice of 2 limes
2 tablespoons *Noilly Prat* vermouth, warmed

Put the egg yolks, mustard, salt, and pepper in a basin and start to whisk gently in one direction only (clockwise or anti-clockwise) — do not change direction.

When the mixture starts to thicken, begin whisking in the oil a drop at a time. As the mixture thickens further, the oil can be added in a very thin stream until it has all been absorbed and the sauce is extremely thick.

Finally, whisk in the lime juice and vermouth.

VARIATIONS

Mayonnaise can be thinned down or lightened by the addition of whipped cream or, preferably, whisked yogurt.

Grainy mustard gives a pleasant texture.

Basil Sauce *(Sauce au Basil)*

To the basic mayonnaise add 1 teaspoon tomato paste (purée), 8 finely chopped basil leaves, 1 crushed garlic clove, and 2 large tablespoons yogurt. Mix well.

Avocado Sauce *(Sauce Avocatine)*

To the basic mayonnaise add ¾ cup (6 oz., 185 g) mashed avocado pulp, ¼ cup (2 fl. oz., 60 ml) low-fat plain yogurt, and a good pinch cayenne pepper. Adjust seasoning.

Pictured on previous pages: Whipped Cream with Mayonnaise,
Saffron Sauce, and Piquant Mint Mayonnaise
Pictured opposite: Provençale Garlic Sauce, and Basil Sauce

Mint Sauce *(Sauce Paloise)*

Blend the basic mayonnaise with 8 fresh mint leaves and ⅓ cup (3 fl. oz., 90 ml) yogurt.

Whipped Cream with Mayonnaise (*Sauce Mousseline*)

Beat ½ cup (4 fl. oz., 125 ml) heavy cream. In another bowl, beat 1 egg white until light and fluffy. Fold both into the basic mayonnaise and check the seasoning.

Brandied Orange Sauce (*Sauce Orangine*)

To the basic mayonnaise add the juice of ½ a blood orange and 2 tablespoons of cognac.

Exotic Sauce (*Sauce Royale*)

Place the basic mayonnaise in a blender or food processor with ¼ cup (1 oz., 30 g) pineapple flesh, 1 teaspoon preserved ginger in its syrup, 1 deseeded chili pepper, 2 tablespoons tomato paste (purée), 1 tablespoon clear honey, and 2 tablespoons either vodka or Marc de Bourgogne. Blend to a smooth sauce and check the seasoning.

Saffron Sauce (*Sauce au Saffran Méridional*)

Brew 5 threads of saffron in 4 tablespoons hot Martini Rosso or Saint Raphaël aperitif for 5 minutes. Blend in a blender or food processor, then beat into the basic mayonnaise along with ½ teaspoon turmeric powder.

Provençale Garlic Sauce (*Sauce Rouille*)

Place the basic mayonnaise in a blender or food processor with 4 chopped garlic cloves, 2 small basil sprigs, 2 teaspoons tomato paste (purée), 1 deseeded red or green chili pepper, and a few threads of saffron. Blend to a smooth purée. Place this sauce in a bowl and beat in ⅓ cup (3 oz., 75 g) hot creamy mashed potato.

This sauce is sometimes made by beating about 1 cup (8 oz., 250 g) garlicky mashed potato in a bowl with 3 sieved, hard-boiled eggs. Then emulsify with at least 1¼ cups (10 fl. oz., 310 ml) olive oil. Season well.

For another variation, place 1 deseeded, chopped red chili pepper and 2 chopped garlic cloves in a blender. Purée, then drizzle in ⅓ cup (3 fl. oz., 90 ml) olive oil as for mayonnaise. Add to 1½ cups (3 oz., 90 g) soft whole-wheat (wholemeal) breadcrumbs to form a stiff purée.

Piquant Mint Mayonnaise (*Sauce Conil*)

Beat together ⅓ cup (5 fl. oz., 155 ml) basic mayonnaise with an equal amount of whipped cream. Stir in 2 tablespoons dry French vermouth and 1 tablespoon French gin. Add 1 tablespoon chopped fresh mint and season generously.

MAKES 2½ CUPS

TARTAR SAUCE

SAUCE TARTARE

1¼ cups (10 fl. oz., 310 ml) basic
mayonnaise (see p. 162)
2 tablespoons chopped capers
4 tablespoons chopped gherkins
1 tablespoon chopped parsley
1 tablespoon chopped tarragon

Stir all the ingredients together to make a well-
blended, even-flavored sauce.
Store, covered, in the refrigerator until required.

SERVES 4

EGG-BASED SAUCES

LES SAUCE AUX OEUFS

I have chosen not to give a definitive master recipe,
although the two egg-based sauces that follow are both,
in their own ways, definitive examples. In fact, hot egg-
based sauces of the type most people know as
'hollandaise' are, to a certain extent, a variation on the
principle of mayonnaise — they rely upon the seemingly
magical ability of eggs to absorb large volumes of oil
to thicken and emulsify the sauce.
For these hot sauces, the acidulating ingredients are
added early in the recipe, and the oil is replaced by
butter, added in tiny pieces, just as the oil is poured in
drop by drop. Great care must be taken to keep the
temperature of the eggs low as too much heat will
obviously result in scrambled — albeit tasty — eggs!

EGG SAUCE WITH VERMOUTH

SAUCE MARSEILLAN

This sauce, from the town where Noilly Prat vermouth is made, is very similar to a béarnaise sauce and epitomizes that type of egg-thickened sauce.

1/3 cup (3 fl. oz., 90 ml) *Noilly Prat* vermouth

2 tablespoons white wine vinegar

1/3 cup (2 oz., 60 g) chopped shallot *or* red onion

1 teaspoon sea salt

1 teaspoon crushed peppercorns

6 egg yolks

8 oz. (250 g) unsalted butter

Put the vermouth and vinegar in a saucepan with the shallot or red onion, salt, and pepper. Boil the liquid until reduced to just 3 tablespoons. Cool and strain.

In a clean saucepan (or the top of a double boiler), beat together the egg yolks and the liquid. Place over another, larger saucepan (or the base of the double boiler) containing simmering water and whisk until the mixture turns pale and thickens to a light custard consistency.

Add the butter bit by bit — you may find it easiest to cut it into about 24 equal cubes before beginning to cook. Beat each piece in well before adding the next. The sauce will thicken and increase in volume to become a creamy, rich, and smooth sauce resembling a hot mayonnaise.

Check throughout the cooking process that the water below the pan does not boil, and do not stop whisking while the eggs are over the hot water. Remove the saucepan from the heat if you are at all worried.

Serve the sauce as soon as the last of the butter has been added and beaten in.

SERVES 4

Pictured left: Tartar Sauce

EGG SAUCE WITH SORREL AND SAMPHIRE

SAUCE À L'OSEILLE ET RAMEAUX DE SALICORNE

This sauce is a delightful variation on the theme of the hot egg-based sauce.

4 oz. (125 g) tender sorrel leaves, picked over, washed, and drained

2 oz. (60 g) samphire, picked over, washed, and drained

5 mint leaves

2/3 cup (5 fl. oz., 155 ml) dry white wine

sea salt and freshly ground black pepper

1 teaspoon clear honey

4 egg yolks

8 oz. (250 g) unsalted butter

1 tablespoon fresh chopped herbs (e.g. mint, sorrel, and chervil), to garnish

Put the sorrel and samphire in a blender or food processor with the wine, salt, pepper, and honey. (Do not add too much salt at this stage as the samphire can be quite salty — it is better to check the seasoning later and add more if necessary then.) Blend to a smooth purée.

Place this mixture in a saucepan and bring to the boil. Boil for about 5 minutes or until reduced by about one-third. Remove from the heat and allow to cool a little.

Beat in the egg yolks. Place the saucepan over another, larger, pan half-filled with hot water and whisk constantly until the mixture starts to lighten and thicken — take care that it does not boil and thus scramble the eggs.

Beat in the butter bit by bit, allowing each piece to be absorbed before adding the next. The sauce will become thick and glossy, with a wonderful color and flavor.

Check the seasoning and serve the sauce warm, sprinkled with fresh herbs.

SERVES 4

BASIC WHITE SAUCE

VELOUTÉ DE NOUVEAU

*This basic white sauce forms the basis for an endless
range of variations, from those flavored with just a few
herbs and spices, to more luxurious ones with cream,
to piquant ones with yogurt, lemon juice, vermouth,
or wine.*

1 oz. (30 g) butter
¼ cup (1 oz., 30 g) whole-wheat (wholemeal) flour *or*
unbleached all-purpose (plain) flour
2½ cups (1 imp. pint, 625 ml) cold vegetable stock
sea salt and freshly ground black pepper

Melt the butter in a pan. Add the flour and
cook gently for just less than a minute. Stir
constantly to avoid the mixture browning. It
should resemble wet sand — this is called a 'roux'.

Gradually whisk in the stock and bring to the
boil, whisking all the time. Cook the sauce gently
for about 5 minutes, so that it thickens to a smooth
cream. Strain and use in your chosen recipe.

Note: This amount will be sufficient for up to
8 portions, depending on its use, and contains only
a few calories per portion.

VARIATIONS

Whisked White Sauce with Vermouth (*Sabayon*)
In a metal bowl, beat together 3 egg yolks and
1 whole egg with 2 tablespoons *Noilly Prat*
vermouth and 2 tablespoons water. Place over a
saucepan of hot water and whisk until the mixture
resembles a thick, frothy custard. Add this to the
basic white sauce.

Cream and Egg Yolk Liaison
Blend 2 egg yolks and 5 tablespoons (2½ fl. oz.,
75 ml) light cream. Beat this mixture into the
white sauce at the last minute, taking care it does
not boil fiercely afterwards.

MAKES 3½ CUPS

*Pictured opposite: Basic White Sauce,
and Rich Onion and Pepper Sauce*

RICH ONION AND PEPPER SAUCE

SAUCE BASQUAISE

¼ cup (2 fl. oz., 60 ml) olive oil
⅓ cup (2 oz., 60 g) chopped onion
⅓ cup (2 oz., 60 g) chopped red and green
sweet pepper (capsicum)
⅔ cup (5 fl. oz., 155 ml) ruby (dark red) port
2 tablespoons tomato paste (purée)
1¼ cup (10 fl. oz., 310 ml) basic white
sauce (this page)

Heat the oil in a saucepan and sauté the onion
and sweet peppers for 3 minutes, stirring to
avoid browning.

Add the port and tomato paste and simmer for
another minute.

Purée this mixture in a blender or food
processor, then return to the saucepan, stir in the
white sauce, and reheat the mixture until boiling.

SERVES 4

WHITE BUTTER SAUCE

BEURRE BLANC

3 tablespoons dry white wine
1 teaspoon lime juice
1 tablespoon *Noilly Prat* vermouth
1 tablespoon chopped shallot
8 oz. (250 g) unsalted butter
sea salt and freshly ground black pepper

Boil together the white wine, lime juice,
vermouth, and shallot for 5 minutes to reduce
the volume by half.

Little by little, add the butter to the hot sauce,
whisking it to form a creamy emulsion. Check the
seasoning. Serve immediately, sprinkled with fresh
chopped herbs of your choice, if desired.

MAKES 1½ CUPS

CLASSIC VINAIGRETTE

LA VINAIGRETTE

There are no set rules for this most simple yet mouth-watering sauce, except that it should be an amalgam of good-quality oil and vinegar or other acetic liquid, such as lemon juice. The balance of these ingredients and whatever else you choose to add to them — a sprinkle of sea salt, freshly ground black pepper, a little sugar or honey, a dab of mustard, crushed garlic, finely chopped fresh or dry herbs — can be varied to suit your tastes and to complement the flavor of the dish the vinaigrette is to accompany.
Here is a basic combination to begin with.

3-4 tablespoons extra-virgin, cold-pressed olive oil
1 tablespoon white wine vinegar
1/2 teaspoon Dijon mustard
pinch of sugar
sea salt and freshly ground black pepper

Using a fork or miniature whisk, beat together the oil and vinegar in a small bowl until they form a smooth emulsion. Whisk in the mustard, then season with sugar, salt, and pepper to taste.

MAKES ½ CUP

CREAMY HORSERADISH SAUCE

SAUCE RAIFORT

1¼ cups (10 fl. oz., 310 ml) basic white
sauce (see p. 166)
1/3 cup (3 fl. oz., 90 ml) light whipping cream
2 tablespoons horseradish cream
1 teaspoon Dijon mustard

Heat the white sauce gently and add all the other ingredients. Stir until smooth and creamy. Serve hot or cold.

SERVES 4

WATERCRESS SAUCE

COULIS DE CRESSON

2 tablespoons butter
1 shallot, chopped
1 garlic clove, crushed
3 oz. (90 g) silken tofu
1/3 cup (3 fl. oz., 90 ml) vegetable stock
1 small bunch watercress, stems discarded
1/2 teaspoon Dijon mustard
sea salt and freshly ground black pepper

Heat the butter in a saucepan and sauté the shallot and garlic for 3 minutes until translucent. Place in a blender or food processor with the tofu, stock, and watercress and blend to a creamy texture.
Return to the saucepan, add the mustard, salt, and pepper, and reheat gently.

SERVES 4

CANTALOUPE AND PORT SAUCE

COULIS DE CANTALOUP AU PORTO BLANC

1½ cups (8 oz., 250 g) diced Cantaloupe (rockmelon)
2 tablespoons white port
1 teaspoon ground ginger
2 tablespoons clear honey
cornstarch (cornflour) and water, to thicken

In a blender or food processor, blend together all the ingredients except the cornstarch.
If a thicker sauce is required, place the purée in a pan and add the appropriate amount of cornstarch dissolved in water. Boil for 4 minutes to stabilize and clear the starch, and leave to cool before serving. This sauce is good with a garnish of wild strawberries.

SERVES 4

Pictured above right: Sauce of Avocado Purée

ALMOND SAUCE

COULIS D'AMANDES

2 cups (8 oz., 250 g) skinned almonds

1¹/3 cups (10 fl. oz., 310 ml) water

1 teaspoon cornstarch (cornflour) (optional)

5 tablespoons (2¹/2 fl. oz., 75 ml) cold water (optional)

¹/4 cup (2 fl. oz., 60 ml) plain yogurt

juice of 1 lemon

1 tablespoon puréed onion *or* garlic *or* ¹/4 cup (2 oz., 60 g) clear honey

In a blender or food processor, blend the almonds and water to a smooth cream. Place in a saucepan and bring to the boil.

Thicken with the cornflour mixed with water if desired, then stir in the yogurt.

Add the lemon juice. Finally, add either the savory or the sweet flavoring, depending on how the sauce is to be used. Heat through and serve.

SERVES 4

SAUCE OF AVOCADO PURÉE

COULIS D'AVOCAT

¹/2 ripe avocado

juice of 1 lemon

¹/4 cup (2 oz., 60 g) fresh tomato pulp

1 garlic clove, crushed

1 tablespoon chopped shallot

pinch of sea salt

pinch of chili powder

1 tablespoon chopped tomato

Put all the ingredients except the chopped tomato into a blender or food processor and blend to a smooth purée.

Transfer to a saucepan and heat through. Just before serving, stir in the chopped tomato for textural and visual appeal.

SERVES 4

TARRAGON SAUCE

SAUCE À L'ESTRAGON

2 tablespoons (1 oz., 30 g) butter
1/4 cup (1 oz., 30 g) whole-wheat (wholemeal) flour
1 1/4 cups (10 fl. oz., 310 ml) milk
sea salt and freshly ground black pepper
freshly grated nutmeg
2 egg yolks
2 eggs, beaten
1/2 cup (2 oz., 60 g) grated Gruyère *or* Cheddar cheese
1 tablespoon each of fresh chopped parsley
and tarragon
juice of 1 lemon

In a saucepan, heat the butter and add the flour to make a roux. Cook without browning for a minute, then add the milk gradually, stirring it in as you go to avoid lumps. Boil gently for 5 minutes. Season with salt, pepper, and nutmeg.

Remove from the heat. Stir in the egg yolks and egg, cheese, parsley, and tarragon. Cool the sauce completely before adding the lemon juice.

SERVES 4

SWEET–SOUR TOMATO SAUCE

COULIS DE TOMATES À L'AIGRE-DOUX

1 lb. (500 g) beefsteak tomatoes, skinned, deseeded,
and chopped
1 shallot, chopped
2 tablespoons chopped red sweet pepper (capsicum)
1/4 cup (2 oz., 60 g) Demerara (raw) sugar
pinch of sea salt
pinch of cayenne pepper
2 tablespoons raspberry vinegar
fresh herbs of choice, snipped

Put the shallot in a pan with the sweet pepper and vinegar. Boil for 2 minutes before adding the sugar, salt, and cayenne pepper. Add the tomato flesh, then simmer for 4 minutes.

Blend in a blender or food processor.

Serve cold, sprinkled with the herbs of your choice. Basil is especially good. For a Provençal touch, a clove of garlic, blended with a tablespoon of olive oil, can be stirred in when the tomatoes are added to the sauce.

SERVES 4

TOMATO DRESSING

COULIS DE TOMATES

1/4 cup (2 fl. oz., 60 ml) olive oil
1 small onion, chopped
1 garlic clove, chopped
8 tomatoes, skinned, deseeded, and chopped
2 tablespoons tomato paste (purée)
1/2 teaspoon sea salt
freshly ground black pepper
1/2 teaspoon Demerara (raw) sugar
1 tablespoon fresh chopped mint and parsley

Heat the oil in a saucepan and sauté the onion for 4 minutes. Add the garlic and cook for a further minute.

Add the tomato and tomato paste. Cook for 4 minutes, stirring, then season to taste with salt, pepper, and sugar. Add the herbs and serve.

SERVES 4

SPICY RED SAUCE

SAUCE ROUGEOLE

1/2 cup (2 fl. oz., 60 ml) vegetable oil
1 garlic clove, chopped
1 red sweet pepper (capsicum), deseeded and chopped
1 lb. (500 g) tomatoes, peeled, deseeded, and diced
2 tablespoons tomato paste (purée)
sea salt
grated nutmeg
large pinch of cayenne pepper *or* 1 fresh chili
pepper, chopped
1 cup (4 oz., 125 g) grated hard cheese, for serving

Heat the oil in a saucepan and stir-fry the garlic and sweet pepper for 4 minutes.

Add the diced tomatoes and cook for a further 3 minutes. Stir in the tomato paste, salt, nutmeg, and cayenne or chili. Heat through, then serve.

SERVES 4

Pictured opposite: Tarragon Sauce, and Sweet–Sour Tomato Sauce

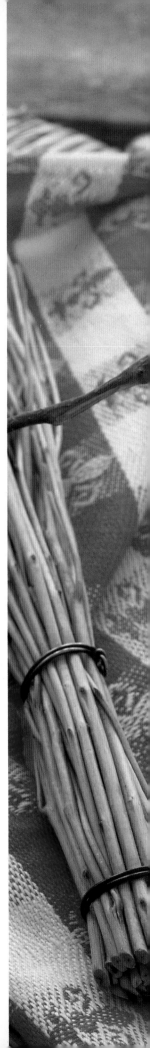

PLUM AND RED WINE SAUCE

COULIS DE PRUNES ROUGES OU NOIRES

1¹/₃ cups (8 oz., 250 g) skinned, pitted black or red
plums (either Victoria or Quetch varieties are suitable)
2 tablespoons Demerara (raw) sugar
¹/₃ cup (3 fl. oz., 90 ml) red wine
1 teaspoon red wine vinegar
1 teaspoon soy sauce
1 garlic clove, crushed
1 teaspoon crushed fresh ginger
cornstarch (cornflour) and water, to thicken

Put the plums in a saucepan with all the
ingredients except the cornstarch and water.
Bring to the boil and then simmer until the plums
are tender.

Purée the mixture in a blender or food
processor, then return to the saucepan and bring
to the boil.

Dissolve the appropriate quantity of cornstarch
in the water. Add to the saucepan and cook for
4 minutes to clear the sauce. Serve hot.

SERVES 4

HERB SAUCE WITH EGG

SAUCE GRIBICHE

4 eggs, hard-boiled and separated
1 teaspoon sea salt
freshly ground black pepper
3 tablespoons white wine vinegar
¹/₂ cup (4 fl oz., 125 ml) olive oil
1 teaspoon Dijon mustard
1 teaspoon each of tarragon, chervil, parsley, capers,
and gherkins, finely chopped
1 scallion (spring onion), chopped

Put the egg yolks in a blender or food processor
with the salt, pepper, vinegar, oil, and
mustard, and blend the ingredients until smooth.

Finely chop the egg whites. Mix them in a bowl
with the sauce and the tarragon, chervil, parsley,
gherkins, capers, and scallion.

Serve chilled.

SERVES 4

SHALLOT CREAM SAUCE

SAUCE RAVIGOTE

1 oz. (30 g) butter
2 tablespoons whole-wheat (wholemeal) flour
5 tablespoons (2¹/₂ fl. oz., 75 ml) water *or*
vegetable stock
5 tablespoons (2¹/₂ fl. oz., 75 ml) light cream
sea salt and freshly ground black pepper
2 tablespoons white wine vinegar
2 tablespoons white wine
2 mushrooms, sliced
1 tablespoon chopped shallot *or* onion
1 bay leaf
cayenne pepper *or* Tabasco (optional)

Heat the butter in a pan and stir in the flour.
Cook for 1 minute without browning.
Gradually pour on the water or stock, stirring all
the time, boil for 4 minutes, then whisk in the
cream. Simmer for 10 minutes. Season with salt
and pepper.

While this white sauce is simmering, put the
remaining ingredients in another saucepan and
boil fiercely until reduced by one-third.

Whisk in the white sauce. Boil for 5 minutes.
Strain. Check the seasoning and add a pinch of
cayenne or a dash of Tabasco, or just extra black
pepper if preferred.

VARIATION
Chopped parsley or other herbs, or chopped sweet
peppers (capsicum), can be added for extra flavor.

SERVES 4

*Pictured opposite: Plum and Red Wine Sauce,
Herb Sauce with Egg, and Shallot Cream Sauce*

INDEX

Numbers in *italics* indicate illustrated dishes.